*Current*
**CONTROVERSIES**

# Immigration

*Debra A. Miller, Book Editor*

**GREENHAVEN PRESS**
*A part of Gale, Cengage Learning*

GALE
CENGAGE Learning

Detroit • New York • San Francisco • New Haven, Conn • Waterville, Maine • London

GALE
CENGAGE Learning

Christine Nasso, *Publisher*
Elizabeth Des Chenes, *Managing Editor*

© 2010 Greenhaven Press, a part of Gale, Cengage Learning

Gale and Greenhaven Press are registered trademarks used herein under license.

*For more information, contact:*
Greenhaven Press
27500 Drake Rd.
Farmington Hills, MI 48331-3535
Or you can visit our Internet site at gale.cengage.com

For product information and technology assistance, contact us at

Gale Customer Support, 1-800-877-4253
For permission to use material from this text or product, submit all requests online at www.cengage.com/permissions

Further permissions questions can be emailed to permissionrequest@cengage.com

Articles in Greenhaven Press anthologies are often edited for length to meet page requirements. In addition, original titles of these works are changed to clearly present the main thesis and to explicitly indicate the author's opinion. Every effort is made to ensure that Greenhaven Press accurately reflects the original intent of the authors. Every effort has been made to trace the owners of copyrighted material.

Cover image copyright © Martyn Goddard/Terra/Corbis.

**LIBRARY OF CONGRESS CATALOGING-IN-PUBLICATION DATA**

Immigration / Debra A. Miller, book editor.
    p. cm. -- (Current controversies)
    Includes bibliographical references and index.
    ISBN 978-0-7377-4709-6 (hardcover) -- ISBN 978-0-7377-4710-2 (pbk.)
    1. United States--Emigration and immigration. 2. United States--Emigration and immigration--Government policy. 3. Illegal aliens--United States. I. Miller, Debra A.
    JV6465.I4717 2010
    325.73--dc22
                                                                2009044185

Printed in the United States of America
1 2 3 4 5 6 7 14 13 12 11 10

# Contents

## Chapter 1: Is Immigration a Serious Problem in the United States?

**Yes: Immigration Is a Serious Problem in the United States**

## Chapter 2: Are Illegal Immigrants Treated Fairly?

## Chapter 3: How Should the U.S. Government Respond to Illegal Immigration?

# Chapter 4: How Should U.S. Immigration Policy Be Reformed?

# Foreword

By definition, controversies are "discussions of questions in which opposing opinions clash" (Webster's Twentieth Century Dictionary Unabridged). Few would deny that controversies are a pervasive part of the human condition and exist on virtually every level of human enterprise. Controversies transpire between individuals and among groups, within nations and between nations. Controversies supply the grist necessary for progress by providing challenges and challengers to the status quo. They also create atmospheres where strife and warfare can flourish. A world without controversies would be a peaceful world; but it also would be, by and large, static and prosaic.

## The Series' Purpose

The purpose of the Current Controversies series is to explore many of the social, political, and economic controversies dominating the national and international scenes today. Titles selected for inclusion in the series are highly focused and specific. For example, from the larger category of criminal justice, Current Controversies deals with specific topics such as police brutality, gun control, white collar crime, and others. The debates in Current Controversies also are presented in a useful, timeless fashion. Articles and book excerpts included in each title are selected if they contribute valuable, long-range ideas to the overall debate. And wherever possible, current information is enhanced with historical documents and other relevant materials. Thus, while individual titles are current in focus, every effort is made to ensure that they will not become quickly outdated. Books in the Current Controversies series will remain important resources for librarians, teachers, and students for many years.

In addition to keeping the titles focused and specific, great care is taken in the editorial format of each book in the series. Book introductions and chapter prefaces are offered to provide background material for readers. Chapters are organized around several key questions that are answered with diverse opinions representing all points on the political spectrum. Materials in each chapter include opinions in which authors clearly disagree as well as alternative opinions in which authors may agree on a broader issue but disagree on the possible solutions. In this way, the content of each volume in Current Controversies mirrors the mosaic of opinions encountered in society. Readers will quickly realize that there are many viable answers to these complex issues. By questioning each author's conclusions, students and casual readers can begin to develop the critical thinking skills so important to evaluating opinionated material.

Current Controversies is also ideal for controlled research. Each anthology in the series is composed of primary sources taken from a wide gamut of informational categories including periodicals, newspapers, books, U.S. and foreign government documents, and the publications of private and public organizations. Readers will find factual support for reports, debates, and research papers covering all areas of important issues. In addition, an annotated table of contents, an index, a book and periodical bibliography, and a list of organizations to contact are included in each book to expedite further research.

Perhaps more than ever before in history, people are confronted with diverse and contradictory information. During the Persian Gulf War, for example, the public was not only treated to minute-to-minute coverage of the war, it was also inundated with critiques of the coverage and countless analyses of the factors motivating U.S. involvement. Being able to sort through the plethora of opinions accompanying today's major issues, and to draw one's own conclusions, can be a complicated and frustrating struggle. It is the editors' hope that Current Controversies will help readers with this struggle.

# Introduction

"America's immigrant population—including both legal and illegal immigrants—reached a record level of 37.9 million in 2007."

The United States has often been called a land of immigrants because of its long history of admitting large numbers of foreign-born people from around the world. These immigrants helped to build the country and infused it with rich cultural diversity. The number of immigrants in the country has spiked dramatically during the last four decades, with the numbers far surpassing even the great waves of immigration that brought millions of Europeans to the United States in the early 1900s. In fact, according to a March 2007 Current Population Survey (CPS) conducted by the U.S. Census Bureau, America's immigrant population—including both legal and illegal immigrants—reached a record level of 37.9 million in 2007. The years since 2000 have seen the highest immigration numbers in U.S. history—more than 10 million new immigrants. As a result, today one out of every eight Americans is an immigrant.

Some of these new immigrants have entered America legally, under various immigration programs set up by the federal government. Under the Immigration and Nationality Act (INA) and its amendments, the nation can give legal permanent resident (LPR or "green card") status to foreign persons who have a close family relationship with a U.S. citizen (spouses, children, parents, or siblings), who have needed job skills, or who are from countries with low levels of immigration to the United States. Another basis for LPR admission is refugee or asylee status—persons who do not want to return to their own country because of persecution or a well-founded fear of persecution on account of race, religion, nationality, membership in a particular social group, or political opinion. The cap on all LPR immigrants under current law is 675,000, but some LPR categories are exempt from this cap, such as the immediate family of U.S. citizens (spouses, children, and parents of citizens over 21 years of age). According to the latest data from the Department of Homeland Security (DHS), 1,107,126 foreigners immigrated here legally as LPRs in 2008. Of those, 716,244 were family-sponsored; 166,511 were employment-based; 166,392 were refugees or asylees; and 15,046 were from other categories. All LPRs can apply for U.S. citizenship once they reside in the country for certain specified periods and if they meet other criteria set forth by U.S. law.

Another way of legally entering the United States under immigration laws is by acquiring a temporary visa. Although not considered immigrants or included in immigration numbers, persons under these programs are permitted to come to the United States for a temporary period—to study, work, represent a foreign government, or for some other business or pleasure. For example, under a program commonly called H-1B, U.S. employers can temporarily (for three to six years) employ foreign workers in specialty occupations such as engineering, math, architecture, physical sciences, biotechnology, medicine, and law. In 2008, DHS estimates that 175 million foreigners—many of whom were tourists and other short-term visitors—entered the country on some type of temporary visa.

Notably, however, illegal immigration accounts for more than half of the post-2000 immigrants to the United States. An illegal immigrant is someone who overstays a temporary visa or enters the United States illegally. Estimates by the Census Bureau and various immigration research organizations consistently indicate that approximately 11 to 12 million illegal immigrants now reside in the United States. Already, these illegal immigrants make up almost one-third of the total U.S. immigrant population. The majority of illegal immigrants are low-skilled and have not completed high school. Most come to this country to find work, although some enter illegally to join family members who have immigrated earlier. Many illegal immigrants work at laborious, low-paying agricultural or manufacturing jobs, but increasingly, immigrants have also begun to work in construction or other occupations where the pay is better. According to the Center for Immigration Studies (CIS), an immigration think tank, the majority of the illegal immigrant population comes from Mexico (57 percent) and Central America (11 percent). Another 9 percent comes from East Asia, 8 percent from South America, and 4 percent from Europe and the Caribbean.

Immigration is one of the biggest drivers of U.S. population growth. Based on census data, CIS has concluded that if immigration continues at current levels, the U.S. population will increase from 301 million today to 468 million in 2060—a 167 million (56 percent) increase. CIS calculates that immigrants and their descendents will account for 105 million (63 percent) of this increase. If immigration levels continue to increase as they have during the last several decades, these numbers could grow even larger. Supporters of lower immigration levels argue that population growth of this magnitude will contribute to more congestion, urban sprawl, traffic, pollution, loss of open spaces, and greenhouse gas emissions.

In addition to increasing the U.S. population, immigration has other effects on the United States, many of which have become fodder for one side or the other in a major debate over U.S. immigration policy. For example, immigration critics claim that immigrants, particularly illegals, are taking jobs from Americans; not paying enough in taxes; creating a burden on government resources due to extra costs for schools, health care, food stamps, and other public benefits; and adding to levels of crime and violence in the United States. Pro-immigration advocates dispute these claims, arguing that illegal immigrants simply do the jobs that Americans will not take, and that they contribute significantly more economically to the United States than they take away in benefits.

The last major reform of U.S. immigration laws came in 1986, in response to the growing numbers of illegal immigrants, when Congress passed the Immigration Reform and Control Act (IRCA). The IRCA granted amnesty to thousands of illegal immigrants residing in the United States at that time, giving them legal status and the right to become U.S. citizens. At the same time, in order to slow the tide of illegal immigration in the future, the IRCA created an employer sanctions program designed to prohibit U.S. employers from hiring illegal workers. Illegal immigration continued and even increased following the passage of the IRCA, and most immigration analysts today admit that the law failed to achieve its purpose of controlling illegal immigration. Many critics blame the government for failing to enforce the employer sanctions contained in the law.

The failure of the 1986 IRCA reforms, and the uptick in illegal immigration during recent years has once again sparked calls for immigration reform. Yet there is still no clear consensus on what's wrong with U.S. immigration policy or how to fix it. The authors of *Current Controversies: Immigration* address some of the questions at the heart of this immigration debate, including whether immigration—legal or illegal—is a serious problem, whether immigrants are treated fairly, how the government should respond to illegal immigration, and how U.S. immigration policies should be reformed.

# Is Immigration a Serious Problem in the United States?

# Chapter Preface

Among the many issues confronting U.S. president Barack Obama is increasing violence from Mexican drug cartels near America's southern border. Since Mexican president Felipe Calderón took office in December 2006, there have been between seven thousand and ten thousand people killed because of wars between rival Mexican drug gangs and between the gangs and the Mexican government. The violence has made for some gruesome headlines: police have been beheaded; government officials and journalists have been targeted; kidnappings have been aimed at ordinary citizens to extort money; and drug gangs are even killing children, breaking traditional codes of honor in Mexico. In addition to this recent explosion of drug violence, Mexico also is battling historic corruption in its law enforcement and judicial institutions—problems that impede the government's efforts to stop the drug-driven chaos.

U.S. policy makers are concerned about the consequences of the Mexican violence for the United States. Many people fear that the drug wars could spill over the border, threatening the security of U.S. border towns, causing injury or death for U.S. police and border patrol agents, or resulting in increased violence within Mexican neighborhoods in U.S. cities. The violence in Mexico could also send Mexican refugees fleeing into the American Southwest, adding to the levels of illegal immigration already flowing into the country. Some commentators have even suggested that, in a worst-case scenario, the cartels could win de facto control over parts of northern Mexico or the Mexican government could completely collapse into civil war, sparking a massive surge of millions of refugees across the border. U.S. officials are already seeing an increase in the numbers of Mexicans who enter the country and request asylum under U.S. immigration laws. And reports suggest that the Mexican cartels routinely follow Mexican targets into the United States to exact their revenge—a trend that is resulting in some level of increased violence in this country. The cartels are also deeply entrenched in smuggling Mexican workers and drugs across the border, and they rely on guns and weapons purchased at U.S. gun shops.

The violence in Mexico has renewed calls in the United States for better border security and immigration reform, but no solution has yet been agreed upon. Obama visited Mexico in April 2009, promising Calderón that he would push for the Senate ratification of a regional arms treaty, but he failed to show support for Calderón's main goal—renewal of a U.S. assault weapons ban that expired in 2004. Mexican government officials think the ban is critical to stopping the flow of guns to the cartels. Others have proposed legalizing marijuana in the United States, since it is one of the main drugs sold by the cartels. Various other solutions offered to Obama, however, directly involve border or immigration issues.

Some groups are pressing the U.S. government to step up immigration enforcement to stem any violence-related increase in illegal immigration into the United States. Other commentators have urged the Department of Homeland Security (DHS) to focus on finding and deporting Mexican criminal elements who may be working with the drug cartels, supplying guns, or carrying out kidnappings or killings in American cities. Meanwhile, Republicans in Congress who represent thirteen border states have urged Obama to complete the border fence planned for certain areas of the southern border. More than six hundred miles of fencing and barriers have already been completed under the authority of earlier legislation, but another seventy miles have yet to be constructed. Civilian border groups, for their part, want to see more of an effort to protect border communities from violence occurring on the Mexican side, whether that means building more fences or sending the National Guard to protect these areas. So far, the United States has only permitted National Guard troops to observe certain border areas, and Obama has indicated a reluctance to militarize the border. The border violence has also given anti-immigration groups ammunition for arguing against any type of amnesty, which would legalize and offer a path to citizenship for the 12 million illegal immigrants believed to be residing in the United States. Many people believe that such an amnesty program, combined with fear of violence in Mexico, could encourage a new wave of illegal immigration, perhaps even larger than the upsurge that occurred following an earlier amnesty program implemented in 1986. On the other side of the issue are commentators who argue that the drug battles are not affecting the United States and that the numbers of immigrants crossing the border from Mexico has declined, not increased, due to the economic recession.

Whatever happens on this issue, the rising levels of violence in Mexico have only added fuel to what was already a contentious debate in the United States about the pros and cons of immigration. The viewpoints in this chapter ask whether immigration—legal and illegal—is a serious problem for the United States.

# Poor Illegal Immigrants Are a Drain on the U.S. Economy

*Byron York*

*Byron York is a White House correspondent for the* National Review, *a conservative political magazine.*

When [President] George W. Bush visited the U.S. Border Patrol's Yuma Station Headquarters in Arizona [in 2007] ... his message on illegal immigration sounded a bit tougher than in the past. "Illegal immigration is a serious problem—you know it better than anybody," he told a group of border agents. "It puts pressure on the public schools and the hospitals, not only here in our border states, but states around the country. It drains the state and local budgets.... Incarceration of criminals who are here illegally strains the Arizona budget. But there's a lot of other ways it strains the local and state budgets. It brings crime to our communities."

The president touted his get-tough-on-the-border policies, enacted under pressure from the then Republican Congress, and singled out Operation Jump Start, under which National Guard troops assist border agents. But he also stressed the need for "comprehensive" reform, and when he did his message sounded like the George W. Bush of old. "Past efforts at reform failed to address the underlying economic reasons behind illegal immigration," the president said. "People are coming here to put food on the table, and they're doing jobs Americans are not doing."

## Illegal Immigrants' Effect on the U.S. Economy

With those words, the president was revisiting the great question in the debate over illegal immigration: Is the presence of illegal immigrants, mostly from Mexico, a boon to the U.S.

Byron York, "What Does Illegal Immigration Cost? A New Study Tries to Nail Down an Answer," *National Review Online*, April 10, 2007. Reproduced by permission.

economy, or a drag? It's a question that has long divided Bush supporters; the *Wall Street Journal* editorial page tells us that a lenient immigration policy is absolutely vital for American prosperity, while enforcement-first advocates tell us a strict policy is the only thing that will ensure continued economic health.

Both have plenty of statistics to cite to make their case. But now a scholar at the Heritage Foundation [a conservative think tank], Robert Rector, has found a new and revealing way to get at the answer.

Rector has just published a study, "The Fiscal Cost of Low-Skill Households to the U.S. Taxpayer," that is ostensibly not about immigration at all. He takes the most detailed look yet at the economics of the 17.7 million American households made up of people without a high school degree. With numbers from the Census Bureau, the Congressional Research Service, the Bureau of Labor Statistics, and other government agencies, Rector found what they make, what they spend, and how much they receive in government services.

---

*In 2004 ... low-skill households received an average of $32,138 per household—the great majority in the form of means-tested aid and direct benefits.*

---

The reason Rector chose to look at low-skilled workers is that it is estimated that nearly two-thirds of illegal immigrants fall into that category. (By way of comparison, slightly less than ten percent of native-born Americans are in that group.) By focusing on those workers, Rector was able to make use of information on them that is more detailed and precise than information on immigrants as a whole. And any conclusions he reached would be applicable to a large majority of illegal immigrants who are already in this country as well as those who would come here under various immigration reform proposals.

Rector began by calculating the dollar value of the benefits those low-skill workers receive from the government. There are direct benefits, like Medicare and Social Security, and means-tested benefits, like food, housing and medical benefits specifically for low-income people. Then there is public education, along with population-based services like police and fire protection, parks, and roads. (Those services benefit everyone, and their cost usually increases as the population increases.) After that, there is interest on the public debts, a burden spread throughout all income groups, and the cost of what Rector calls "pure public goods"—national defense, scientific research, and a few other areas—which benefit everyone but do not necessarily rise in cost as the population rises.

## Rector's Findings

Rector found that in 2004, the most recent year for which figures are available, low-skill households received an average of $32,138 per household—the great majority in the form of means-tested aid and direct benefits. (Rector excluded from that figure the cost of public goods and interest; with those included, he says, each low-skill household receives an average of $43,084.) Against that, Rector found that low-skill households paid an average of $9,689 in taxes. (The biggest chunk of that was the Social Security tax—$2,509—followed by state and local taxes, consumption taxes, property taxes, and federal income taxes, but Rector counted everything, including highway levies and lottery purchases.) In the final calculation, he found, the average low-skill household received $22,449 more in benefits than it paid in taxes—the $32,138 in benefits, excluding public goods, minus the $9,689 in taxes.

Taking that $22,449, and multiplying it by the 17.7 million low-skill households, Rector found that the total deficit for such households was $397 billion in 2004. "Over the next ten years the total cost of low-skill households to the taxpayer (immediate benefits minus taxes paid) is likely to be at least

$3.9 trillion," Rector writes. "This number would go up significantly if changes in immigration policy lead to substantial increases in the number of low-skill immigrants entering the country and receiving services."

---

*Over the next ten years the total cost of low-skill households to the taxpayer . . . is likely to be at least $3.9 trillion.*

---

From a purely money perspective, it's a powerful argument. At a cost of $22,449 per household per year—well, multiply that by an adult lifespan of 50 years and you have an average lifetime cost to the taxpayer of $1.1 million per unskilled worker. Increase that population with a wave of unskilled immigrants, and you're talking a lot of money.

## Room for Argument

There's probably room for argument on Rector's exact numbers. Jeffrey Passel, a senior research associate at the Pew Hispanic Center, questions whether some of Rector's cost estimates might be too high. For example, the arrival of new illegal immigrations will likely not raise the cost of defending the country, he says, so perhaps future immigrants will not be quite as expensive as Rector claims. (Rector tried to address that issue by excluding the cost of pure public goods in the $22,449 figure.) Still, Passel does not question the basic premise of Rector's report. "One of the purposes of our government is to provide support for people on the low end," says Passel. "Of course there is a bit more spending on households on the lower end than on the high end, and of course the low-income households don't pay as much as the high-income households. That's not surprising."

The bigger argument over Rector's approach is whether illegal immigrants bring economic benefits that outweigh their undisputed costs. Tamar Jacoby, an advocate of comprehensive reform who is a senior fellow at the Manhattan Institute, points to a study done recently of immigrants in North Carolina which estimated that in the past ten years Hispanic immigrants had cost the state $61 million in benefits while being responsible for more than $9 billion in economic growth. "Yes, the individual might cost more in services," says Jacoby, "but they are growing the pie so significantly that that cost pales in comparison."

Not so, says Rector. "The problem is, the growth to the pie that they make, they eat," he explains. The economic growth reflected in the numbers, he says, is what the immigrant workers are making. "To the extent that they make the pie grow any bit more than what they take out of the pie in wages, it is very subtle, and it would be a tiny fraction of the gross domestic product growth," Rector says.

And that means something for the immigration debate. . . . "Every one of these [reform] bills envisions bringing in millions and millions of additional low-skill immigrants with the right to access welfare and become citizens," says Rector. "Within ten years, you would have four million of these individuals, each of whom can bring family. You'd be looking at a cost of $80 billion per year." Perhaps Congress and the president will decide to do that. But if Robert Rector is correct, no one should underestimate the cost.

# Illegal Immigration Threatens U.S. Security

## Tim Kane and Kirk A. Johnson

*Tim Kane is a fellow in labor policy and Kirk A. Johnson is a senior policy analyst in the Center for Data Analysis at the Heritage Foundation, a conservative think tank.*

Illegal immigration into the United States is massive in scale. More than 10 million undocumented aliens currently reside in the United States, and that population is growing by 700,000 per year. On one hand, the presence of so many aliens is a powerful testament to the attractiveness of America. On the other hand, it is a sign of how dangerously open our borders are.

---

*Illegal immigration into the United States is massive in scale.*

---

## The Real Threat—Security

Typical illegal aliens come to America primarily for better jobs and in the process add value to the U.S. economy. However, they also take away value by weakening the legal and national security environment. When three out of every 100 people in America are undocumented (or, rather, documented with forged and faked papers), there is a profound security problem. Even though they pose no direct security threat, the presence of millions of undocumented migrants distorts the law, distracts resources, and effectively creates a cover for terrorists and criminals.

In other words, the real problem presented by illegal immigration is security, not the supposed threat to the economy.

Indeed, efforts to curtail the economic influx of migrants actually worsen the security dilemma by driving many migrant workers underground, thereby encouraging the culture of illegality. A noncitizen guest worker program is an essential component of securing the border, but only if it is the right program.

---

*An honest assessment acknowledges that illegal immigrants bring real benefits to the supply side of the American economy.*

---

It is important to craft a guest worker program intelligently. While there are numerous issues involved in such a program, many of which are beyond the scope of this paper, the evidence indicates that worker migration is a net plus economically. With this in mind, there are 14 principles—with an eye toward the economic incentives involved—that should be included as part of a guest worker program.

## Immigration Benefits and Costs

An honest assessment acknowledges that illegal immigrants bring real benefits to the supply side of the American economy, which is why the business community is opposed to a simple crackdown. There are economic costs as well, given America's generous social insurance institutions. The cost of securing the border would logically exist regardless of the number of immigrants.

The argument that immigrants harm the American economy should be dismissed out of hand. The population today includes a far higher percentage (12 percent) of foreign-born Americans than in recent decades, yet the economy is strong, with higher total gross domestic product (GDP), higher GDP per person, higher productivity per worker, and more Americans working than ever before. Immigration may not have caused this economic boom, but it is folly to blame immigrants for hurting the economy at a time when the economy is simply not hurting. As Stephen Moore pointed out in a recent [2005] article in the *Wall Street Journal*:

> The increase in the immigration flow has corresponded with steady and substantial reductions in unemployment from 7.3 percent to 5.1 percent over the past two decades. And the unemployment rates have fallen by 6 percentage points for blacks and 3.5 percentage points for Latinos.

Whether low-skilled or high-skilled, immigrants boost national output, enhance specialization, and provide a net economic benefit. The 2005 *Economic Report of the President* (ERP) devotes an entire chapter to immigration and reports that, "A comprehensive accounting of the benefits and costs of immigration shows the benefits of immigration exceed the costs." The following are among the ERP's other related findings:

- Immigrant unemployment rates are lower than the national average in the United States;

- Studies show that a 10 percent share increase of immigrant labor results in roughly a 1 percent reduction in native wages—a very minor effect;

- Most immigrant families have a positive net fiscal impact on the United States, adding $88,000 more in tax revenues than they consume in services; and

- Social Security payroll taxes paid by improperly identified (undocumented) workers have led to a $463 billion funding surplus.

## The Argument for Skilled Immigration

The macroeconomic argument in favor of immigration is especially compelling for highly educated individuals with backgrounds in science, engineering, and information technology. The increasing worry about outsourcing jobs to other nations is just one more reason to attract more jobs to America by in-sourcing labor. If workers are allowed to work inside the United States, they immediately add to the economy and pay taxes, which does not happen when a job is outsourced. There-fore, capping the number of H-1B [allows employers to hire foreign workers for specialty occupations on a temporary ba-sis] visas limits America's power as a brain "magnet" attracting highly skilled workers, thereby weakening U.S. firms' competi-tiveness.

Congress increased the number of H-1B visas by 20,000 in November 2004 after the annual cap was exhausted on the first day of fiscal year (FY) 2005. On August 12, 2005, the U.S. Citizenship and Immigration Services announced that it had already received enough H-1B applications for FY 2006 (which began October 1, 2005) and would not be accepting any more applications for the general selection lottery. These and other numbers show that more workers from abroad, not fewer, are needed.

## Low-Skill Immigration Effects

Still, critics of this type of insourcing worry that jobs are be-ing taken away from native-born Americans in favor of low-wage foreigners. Recent data suggest that these fears are over-blown. While the nation's unemployment rate generally has remained just above 5 percent over the past year [2005–2006], unemployment in information technology now stands at a four-year low of 3.7 percent.

While the presence of low-skill migrant workers can be construed as a challenge to low-skill native workers, the eco-nomic effects are the same as the effects of free trade—a net positive and a leading cause of economic growth. A National Bureau of Economic Research study by David Card found that "Overall, evidence that immigrants have harmed the opportunities of less educated natives is scant." The consensus of the vast majority of economists is that the broad economic gains from openness to trade and immigration far outweigh the isolated cases of economic loss. In the long run, as has been documented in recent years, the gains are even higher.

---

*The real problem with undocumented immigrant workers is that flouting the law has become the norm, which makes the job of terrorists and drug traffickers infinitely easier.*

---

A simple example is instructive in terms of both trade and immigration. An imaginary small town has 10 citizens: some farmers, some ranchers, a fisherman, a tailor, a barber, a cook, and a merchant. A new family headed by a young farmer moves to town. His presence is resented by the other farmers, but he also consumes from the other business in town—getting haircuts, eating beef and fish, having his shirts sewn and pressed, and buying supplies at the store, not to mention paying taxes. He undoubtedly boosts the supply side of the economy, but he also boosts the demand side. If he were run out of town for "stealing jobs," his demand for everyone's work would leave with him.

The real problem with undocumented immigrant workers is that flouting the law has become the norm, which makes the job of terrorists and drug traffickers infinitely easier. The economic costs of terrorism can be very high and very real, quite apart from the otherwise positive economic impact of immigration. In order to separate the good from the bad, there is no substitute for a nationwide system that identifies all foreign persons present within the United States. It is not sufficient to identify visitors upon entry and exit; rather, all foreign visitors must be quickly documented.

# Economic Principles for an Effective Guest Worker Program

To this end, 14 economic principles should be borne in mind in crafting an effective guest worker program:

1. All guest workers in the United States should be identified biometrically. . . .

2. Existing migrant workers should have incentives to register with the guest worker program. . . .

3. U.S. companies need incentives to make the program work. . . .

4. Guest worker status should not be a path to citizenship and should not include rights to U.S. social benefits. . . .

5. Efficient legal entry for guest workers is a necessary condition for compliance. . . .

6. Efficient legal entry should be contingent upon a brief waiting period. . . .

7. Provisions for efficient legal entry will not be amnesty. . . .

8. Government agencies should not micromanage migrant labor. . . .

9. The guest worker program should not be used as an excuse to create another large federal bureaucracy. . . .

10. Bonds should be used to promote compliance after entry. . . .

11. Guest workers should be required to find a sponsoring employer. . . .

12. Day laborers should be required to find long-term sponsoring employers. . . .

# tinuing to Allow
# s Legal Immigration
# l Exhaust U.S.
# ural Resources

*Wooldridge*

*Wooldridge is a journalist, writer, environmentalist, trav-*
*id a prominent figure in the U.S. anti-illegal immigration*
*ient.*

hile the immigration debate rages across the planet,
most authorities, leaders and the media tremble at the
)n of hyper-immigration growth, "widely recognized as
·r component of the social, economic and environmen-
blems facing mankind."

us examine a man on the forefront of the immigration
'acing the United States of America. His seminal work
itinues as the single most compelling catalyst for dis-
1 on what America faces in the 21st century.

1 1975, Dr. John Tanton's essay entitled 'International
ion' placed third in the Mitchell Prize competition. The
was given during the 'Limits to Growth Conference' in
ands, Texas. The conference was sponsored by the Club
ne, the University of Houston and Mitchell Energy &
·pment Corporation. The paper became the cover story
: *Ecologist* in July 1976. It planted the seed from which
ration reform germinated. While Tanton's subsequent
3s reveal a deeper insight, none is more prescient or
," said John Rohe, publisher.

ile most Americans docilely accept 1.2 million legal
rants into the United States annually, they don't quite
tand the long-term ramifications facing their progeny

ooldridge, "U.S. Faces Immigration Nightmare in 2009," Rense.com, December
Reproduced by permission of the author.

13. Migrants and employers who do
    new law should be punished. . . .

14. All migrants should respect Am
    traditions. . . .

The century of globalization will
scend into timid isolation or affirm its
history, great nations have declined
walls of insularity, but America has
over a century. It would be a tragedy i
toward a false sense of security just w
with openness, Western Europe is decli
the real solution is so obvious from o
tage.

**Co**
**Ma**
**Wil**
**Nat**

*Frost*

*Frost*
*eler, a*
*move*

W

ment
a ma
tal pr
L
crisis
. . . c
cussi
"
Migr
awar
Woo
of R
Deve
for t
imm
writi
pivot
V
imm
unde

Frosty
29, 20(

as water, energy and resources exhaust themselves from sheer over-use and over-extension.

That same 1.2 million annual immigration pattern added 100 million in the past 40 years. Continuing that mass immigration guarantees an added 100 million people to the United States by 2035. For all U.S. citizens, it portends a crisis-filled future, i.e., water shortages, energy, accelerating pollution, species extinction, quality of life and many other issues.

## A Lack of Media Coverage

"The spatial distribution of human populations is importantly related to such phenomena as urban areas insufficiently dense for mass transit and loss of prime agricultural land to development," Tanton said. "Conspicuous by its absence from the environmental literature, however, is the role international migration plays in the demographic and other problems facing mankind."

*Mexico expects to grow from 108 million in 2009 to 153 million in 2050—a scant 41 years from now.*

Even with Anderson Cooper and Lisa Ling, of CNN's *Planet in Peril*, visiting the most horribly contaminated and dangerous places on Earth, they fail to mention human overpopulation! Ling quoted the astounding fact that humans kill 100 million sharks annually for nothing more than their dorsal fins to feed, as a delicacy, Japanese and Chinese palates. That 100 million shark deaths annually has transpired for 20 years! Ling also reported that 200,000 elephants in one African preserve in the Congo suffered poaching down to their present number of 2,900—in the last 30 years. Bandits slaughter those elephants for nothing more than their two ivory tusks.

Tanton's paper touched the tip of the iceberg in 1975, which, today manifests in greater drama since we grew from

4.0 billion to our present 6.7 billion—on our way to 9.8 billion in 40 years—net gain of another 3.1 billion people.

"It is, however, no more inconsistent for the offspring of immigrants to consider the limitation of immigration than it is for the products of conception to plan to limit births or the beneficiaries of past economic growth to consider limitations," Tanton said. "Mexico is one source of illegal migrants to the United States. The driving force behind the migration northward is the great disparity in employment opportunity and income between the two nations."

Let us understand that Mexico expects to grow from 108 million in 2009 to 153 million in 2050—a scant 41 years from now. All of Latin America expects to double from its 325 million to well over 650 million within 40 years. Imagine CNN's *Planet in Peril* subject lines in four decades; much worse than 2008!

## Dealing with Mass Migration

When talented and educated third world citizens migrate to other countries, they leave a brain drain and loss of leadership abilities. "Illegal immigration is at least a stepchild of the brain drain, for it is increasing the economic disparity between nations that is the chief impetus behind this phenomenon," Tanton said. "The world population problem cannot be solved by mass international migration. If developed nations took in the annual growth of the less developed nations, they would have to accommodate 53 million persons annually. This would give them an annual growth rate of 6.3 percent and a doubling time of eleven years. In the face of this impossibility, the main avenue open for the developed nations to help the less developed ones is to restrict their own growth and to seek to apply the resources thus conserved to the solution of the problems of the less developed nations."

In 2009, a brilliantly inept U.S. Congress, led by myopic Senator Harry Reid and indolent House Majority Speaker Nancy Pelosi expect to ram an immigration amnesty that will not only allow 20 to 30 million illegal alien migrants instant citizenship, but they also expect to continue 'chain migration' and double legal immigration from its current 1.2 million to 2.4 million per year. That action will add 100 million people to the United States within 30 years.

---

*Mass migration will prove America's most daunting dilemma. It will not survive endless massive immigration.*

---

"The question we face is not whether immigration should be restricted, for it has been for decades in all countries," Tanton said. "Rather, the question is, what restrictions are appropriate to today's world? Reexamination of this question is made easier by the realization that current limits are arbitrary in their origins. Many were set decades ago without consideration of population, resource, environmental, and other facts that can and should be taken into account today.

"Happily, it is possible to envision a world in which international migration could become free and unfettered. Appropriately, it is the world of a stationary state, in which people in different regions are in equilibrium with resources, and in which there is a reasonable chance in each region for self-fulfillment, matched with social equity. Under these conditions, international migration could be unfettered, because there would be little incentive to move. Contentment with conditions at home, coupled with man's strong attachment to things familiar, would serve to keep most people in place. While the freedom to migrate at will is incompatible with the physical realities of today's world, it is one of many things that can be restored as man achieves balance with his environment."

While Dr. Tanton espoused such a world in 1975 with a world population of 4.0 billion, humanity faces 6.7 billion today and growing by 77 million desperately poor annually—net gain.

Their main destinations? Functioning democracies in Europe and the United States! Mass migration will prove America's most daunting dilemma. It will not survive endless massive immigration.

Reasonable solution: full out moratorium on all immigration into the Unites States! After a five- to ten-year moratorium, a maximum of 100,000 annually, only if that many egress America each year. President Obama must understand that no solutions can work if we add 2.4 million immigrants annually into our country without end. We must move toward a stable, sustainable and balanced civilization.

Otherwise, as Dr. Tanton observes, the United States and her citizens face a world of hurt in the coming decade.

# Legal Immigration Is More of a Problem than Illegal Immigration

*Edwin S. Rubenstein*

*Edwin S. Rubenstein is an economic journalist and president of ESR Research Economic Consultants in Indianapolis, Indiana.*

Everyone is against illegal immigration (they say). Problem: legal immigration is actually the bigger problem.

## Comparing Numbers

How many legal immigrants enter the United States each year? Let me count the ways they come in . . .

The 1990 immigration law "capped" legal immigration at 700,000 persons a year. Yet since 1990, there've been only two years in which legal immigration has been below that level.

In 2006, 1,266,264 people were granted legal permanent resident status. That's a record if you exclude the post-IRCA [Immigration Reform and Control Act of 1986] amnesty spike of the early 1990s—which reflected the 1986 amnestying of illegal aliens already here.

In contrast, the stock of illegals in the United States is growing by an estimated 500,000/year.

There are about 26 million legal immigrants in the country. Notoriously, the U.S. government doesn't know how many illegals are here. The official estimate is 12 million, but it could be as high as 20 million. This is certainly a scandalous situation. But, either way, there are still more legal immigrants—and their numbers are growing faster.

## Legal Loopholes

Why doesn't the 1990 "cap" on legal immigration work? Because it exempts "immediate family" of U.S. citizens. Current immigration law allows both naturalized and U.S.-born citizens to bring in their spouses, children and parents without limit—a never-ending chain. Legal residents (i.e., green card holders), may have to wait several years before bringing their families to America (legally). But of course, once they're here, they're here.

The "immediate family" loophole accounted for 580,483 immigrants in 2006, slightly less than half of all legal immigrants admitted that year. Over the past decade it has been the largest category of legal immigrant admissions.

About half of all legal immigrants were already in the country prior to becoming a "legal immigrant" through various maneuvers.

One way in which this can happen arises out of the current misinterpretation of the "citizen child" clause of the Fourteenth Amendment. A child born to an illegal alien in the United States is automatically a U.S. citizen—an "anchor baby." In the present climate, this means the parents are hard to deport as a practical matter—and the child will be able to petition his parents into the United States legally when he reaches 18. (An estimated 300,000 "anchor babies" are born in California each year.)

Or an illegal alien can marry a U.S. citizen. (An Asian marriage ring was recently broken up by the ICE [Immigration and Customs Enforcement]—one woman, Julie Tran, pled guilty to being involved in "as many as 75 sham marriages," a scam to get green cards for both local and overseas clients.)

Refugees are another category exempt from the worldwide limit. A refugee is defined as "an alien outside the United

States who is unable or unwilling to return to his or her country of nationality because of persecution or a well-founded fear of persecution."

A sister category—asylee—refers to such people who have somehow already gotten into the United States.

Any Somali or Hmong can show up at a Catholic charity intake office in Mogadishu or Bangkok and be processed as a refugee.

The refugee and asylee categories are just another form of expedited immigration. As Peter Brimelow points out in [his book] *Alien Nation*, more than 80% of refugees have relatives already here—something that would be impossible if these individuals had truly been selected at random from disenfranchised peoples.

216,454 refugees and asylees were admitted in 2006.

The "diversity lottery" is another end-run around immigration laws. It allows millions of people around the world to send in an electronic lottery number from which 50,000 winners are picked each year.

Since no ties to relatives in the United States are required, the program was supposed to allow a more geographically diverse group of people to obtain permanent resident status.

---

*Legal immigration is larger, growing faster, potentially more disruptive [than illegal immigration]—and, because it is set by inflexible statute, just as much out of control.*

---

It hasn't worked. Most winning lottery tickets are eventually disqualified because of fraud—many individuals sending in multiple entries under different aliases. And the winners are disproportionately from the Muslim world—with several implicated in terrorism in the United States.

## Guest Worker Programs

And then there are legal "nonimmigrants," a group that includes H-1Bs [those foreigners who are temporarily hired by employers for a specialty occupation] who are admitted because their high-tech skills are in short supply. H-1Bs are capped at 65,000. But a whopping 407,418 were actually admitted in 2006.

That's because the "cap" pertains only to persons working in the private sector. Universities and nonprofits can apply for an unlimited number of H-1Bs—even though most of these "exempt" H-1Bs eventually get green cards and become naturalized citizens.

Another guest worker program, the H-2B, admits persons who "perform services unavailable in the United States" They're mainly seasonal workers in tourist areas and construction sites. This program is also "capped" at 66,000 per year. But—as with its H-1B cousin—the cap exempts students and individuals working for nonprofits. 87,000 H-2Bs were admitted in 2004, the latest year of available data.

And in case you're wondering, the anchor baby loophole applies to guest workers also. H-1Bs and H-2Bs are allowed to bring in spouses (and children). These are not counted towards the "cap." And, as with illegal aliens, a baby born here means they are hard to deport and can ultimately be sponsored in by their citizen child.

The legal immigration problem has dropped off America's radar screen—displaced by the undeniable crisis over illegals.

But legal immigration is larger, growing faster, potentially more disruptive—and, because it is set by inflexible statute, just as much out of control.

# Both Legal and Illegal Immigrants Help the U.S. Economy

*Alan Greenspan*

*Alan Greenspan is an economist and was the chairman of the Federal Reserve of the United States from 1987 to 2006.*

Immigration to the United States slowed markedly with the onset of the current economic crisis. But as this crisis fades, there is little doubt that the attraction of the United States to foreign workers and their families will revive. I hope by then a badly needed set of reforms to our nation's immigration laws will have been put in place.

## Economic Benefits from Illegal Immigrant Workers

There are two distinctly different policy issues that confront the Congress. The first is illegal immigration. The notion of rewarding with permanent resident status those who have broken our immigration laws does not sit well with the American people. In a recent poll, two-thirds would like to see the number of illegals decreased.

But there is little doubt that unauthorized, that is, illegal, immigration has made a significant contribution to the growth of our economy. Between 2000 and 2007, for example, it accounted for more than a sixth of the increase in our total civilian labor force. The illegal part of the civilian labor force diminished last year [2008] as the economy slowed, though illegals still comprised an estimated 5% of our total civilian labor force. Unauthorized immigrants serve as a flexible compo-

Alan Greenspan, Testimony of Dr. Alan Greenspan Before the Senate Subcommittee on Immigration, Refugees, and Border Security, U.S. Senate, Committee on the Judiciary, April 30, 2009. Reproduced by permission of the author.

nent of our workforce, often a safety valve when demand is pressing and among the first to be discharged when the economy falters.

Some evidence suggests that unskilled illegal immigrants (almost all from Latin America) marginally suppress wage levels of native-born Americans without a high school diploma, and impose significant costs on some state and local governments.

However, the estimated wage suppression and fiscal costs are relatively small, and economists generally view the overall economic benefits of this workforce as significantly outweighing the costs. Accordingly, I hope some temporary worker program can be crafted.

## The Need for Skilled Immigrant Workers

The second policy issue that must be addressed by Congress is the even more compelling need to facilitate the inflow of skilled foreign workers. Our primary and secondary school systems are increasingly failing to produce the skilled workers needed to utilize fully our ever more sophisticated and complex stock of intellectual and physical capital. This capital stock has been the critical input for our rising productivity and standards of living and can be expected to continue to be essential for our future prosperity. The consequence of our educational shortfall is that a highly disproportionate number of our exceptionally skilled workers are foreign-born—two-fifths of the science PhDs in our workforce, for example, are foreign-born. Silicon Valley has a remarkably large number of foreign-born workers.

The quantity of temporary H-1B [allows employers to hire foreigners for specialty occupations on a temporary basis] visas issued each year is far too small to meet the need, especially in the near future as the economy copes with the forthcoming retirement wave of skilled baby boomers. As Bill Gates, the chairman of Microsoft, succinctly testified before Congress in March 2007, "America will find it infinitely more difficult to maintain its technological leadership if it shuts out the very people who are most able to help us compete." He added that we are "driving away the world's best and brightest precisely when we need them most."

---

*There is little doubt that ... illegal immigration has made a significant contribution to the growth of our economy.*

---

Our skill shortage, I trust, will ultimately be resolved through reform of our primary and secondary education systems. But, at best, that will take many years. An accelerated influx of highly skilled immigrants would bridge that gap and, moreover, carry with it two significant bonuses.

First, skilled workers and their families form new households. They will, of necessity, move into vacant housing units, the current glut of which is depressing prices of American homes. And, of course, house price declines are a major factor in mortgage foreclosures and the plunge in value of the vast quantity of U.S. mortgage-backed securities that has contributed substantially to the disabling of our banking system. The second bonus would address the increasing concentration of income in this country. Greatly expanding our quotas for the highly skilled would lower wage premiums of skilled over lesser skilled. Skill shortages in America exist because we are shielding our skilled labor force from world competition. Quotas have been substituted for the wage pricing mechanism. In the process, we have created a privileged elite whose incomes are being supported at noncompetitively high levels by immigration quotas on skilled professionals. Eliminating such restrictions would reduce at least some of our income inequality.

If we are to continue to engage the world and enhance our standards of living, we will have to either markedly improve our elementary and secondary education or lower our barriers to skilled immigrants. In fact, progress on both fronts would confer important economic benefits.

## A Source of Strength

Immigration policy, of course, is influenced by far more than economics. Policy must confront the very difficult issue of the desire of a population to maintain the cultural roots that help tie a society together. Clearly a line must be drawn between, on the one hand, allowing the nation to be flooded with immigrants that could destabilize the necessary comity of a society and, on the other hand, allowing the nation to become static and bereft of competition, and as a consequence to lose its economic vitality. The United States has always been able eventually to absorb waves of immigration and maintain its fundamental character as a nation, particularly the individual rights and freedoms bestowed by our Founding Fathers. But it must be conceded that the transitions were always more difficult than hindsight might now make them appear.

In closing, I would like to concur with President Bill Clinton's view of our immigration history as expressed in remarks of more than a decade ago: "America has constantly drawn strength and spirit from wave after wave of immigrants. . . . They have proved to be the most restless, the most adventurous, the most innovative, the most industrious of people."

We, as a nation, must continue to draw on this source of strength and spirit. To do so, in the context of a rapidly changing global economy, our immigration laws must be reformed and brought up to date.

# Markets Solve the Immigration "Problem"

*John Tamny*

*John Tamny is a senior economist with H.C. Wainwright & Co. Economics. He also is editor of RealClearMarkets, a business news Web site, and writes a weekly column for* Forbes, *an American financial magazine.*

During the darkest days of the war in Iraq, former British Prime Minister Tony Blair was asked whether the United States' best days were behind it. Instead of piling on with the popular suggestion that the United States was a nation in decline, Blair calmly replied that failing countries usually repel rather than attract immigrants.

Far from indicating a country on the ropes, the foreigners seeking both legal and illegal entry into the United States in the last decade are a market signal pointing to a nation doing far better than elite thinking around the world has suggested. Simply put, countries that attract the washed and unwashed the world over are pictures of success; the countries that lose their limited human capital are failures. Cuba, North Korea and Zimbabwe do not have immigration "problems."

Blair's past thinking takes on new meaning when we consider a recent front page story from *USA Today* titled, "Fewer Immigrants Caught Sneaking into U.S." Thanks to a weakened economic outlook stateside, the number of people "caught trying to sneak into the USA from Mexico is at its lowest level since the mid-1970s."

No doubt tougher border enforcement explains some of the above, but the bigger story here reveals the market forces that factor into all human activity. With jobs in the U.S. presently harder to come by, the number of migrants here has declined. As University of Texas, El Paso professor Josiah Heyman described it to *USA Today*, when economic opportunities in the United States become less plentiful, "Word gets back to Mexico really fast."

---

*The United States does not have an "immigration problem."*

---

All of this speaks to a broader truth about immigration itself. High immigration doesn't indicate a nation besieged, but rather the fact that jobs exist. When jobs do not exist, basic market forces cause migrants to seek economic opportunity elsewhere.

The United States does not have an "immigration problem." It would be more realistic to say that for much of the last 25 years the United States has been blessed with a booming economy; one made more vibrant thanks to the influx of workers seeking better opportunity in an economy that needed more workers than our existing population provided. In *The Wealth of Nations*, Adam Smith used a pin factory to show the wonders of the division of labor, and in our case, new human capital from across the border has freed us up to do even higher value work during a period mostly marked by labor shortages, as opposed to labor gluts.

So if it's established that the somewhat natural ups and downs of our economy serve as a natural, market-driven regulator of worker inflows into the states, this reality should cause us to rethink policies meant to keep immigrants from reaching the United States altogether. As the aforementioned downturn has revealed, worker demand, or lack thereof, does a good job in that regard.

More broadly, the problem with making natural migration toward economic opportunity illegal is that it creates negative incentives. Thanks to tough border enforcement, the incentive exists for immigrants to hide their labor once they've made it across the border. And due to very real uncertainty with regard to returning if they leave, illegal immigrants are more likely to bring their families than they would if their passage were legal. According to a 2006 *Wall Street Journal* article by Joel Millman, those whose work is legal aren't as likely to become full-time residents. Instead, when labor shortages in the United States reveal themselves, these workers legally cross the border until the work that brought them here is done. They then return home until the next opportunity in the states arises.

As Millman wrote, not only are these situational workers "a boon to employers," they also "rarely put a burden on social services, because they leave their school-age children and elderly relatives at home." And unlike undocumented workers, who, according to Millman, "are less likely to pay taxes," these legal workers from Mexico generally "pay all state, local and federal taxes," not to mention that they're covered by workmans' compensation as a result of "paying into a fund covering all workers on the job."

---

*The ambition [of migrants] ... is our treasure, one that enriches us given the simple truth that workers are capital, and their efforts add to our national wealth.*

---

Some would argue that lax policing of our borders is a non-starter during a time when terrorists are devising all manner of ways to get into the country. It's a good point, but it merely speaks to the importance of making all work in the United States legal. Rather than sneaking across the border, potential laborers would have every incentive to report their arrival *at* the border. This alone would make those looking to cross undetected conspicuous in their attempt at stealth, and more readily detectable by border patrol agents freed up to deter activity that is actually criminal.

Another anti-immigration argument says that rather than accepting Mexican labor, U.S. authorities should demand that Mexico change the antigrowth policies there that make the United States a magnet for its citizens to begin with. A fair point for sure, but also an excellent endorsement of policies stateside meant to make worker inflows legal. Indeed, when Mexicans leave their country for the United States, Mexico is not just losing a large percentage of its population, but more important, some of its most industrious citizens. If work here were made legal, Mexican politicians, faced with the loss of some of their best and brightest, would finally be forced to address the policies that regularly drive its citizens to better economic climes.

But until the day comes that Mexico liberalizes its economy, the United States would do best to embrace the words of 19th century political economist Jean-Baptiste Say. In writing about immigration, Say observed, "A nation, receiving a stray child into its bosom again acquires a real treasure." Looked at from our perspective, when people migrate to the United States, the ambition that brings them here is our treasure, one that enriches us given the simple truth that workers are capital, and their efforts add to our national wealth.

# Xenophobia Is a Bigger Problem than Illegal Immigration

*Michael Brandon Harris-Peyton*

*Michael Brandon Harris-Peyton is a student at Drexel University in Pennsylvania, majoring in English and Japanese.*

It is a sad day in United States history when some politician thinks that we can solve illegal immigration with a fence. Fences will not solve the problem. It might, however, cut through American towns, as the most recent plans for a border fence in Texas, along the Rio Grande would. The no-man's-land between the fences and the border would contain the U.S.-side banks of the river, including a number of backyards and houses. Illegal immigration prevention, right in your living room. Literally.

## Other Inadequate Solutions

The proposed solution to illegal immigrants simply cutting through or hopping the fence would be cameras. But you have to pay people to watch cameras, and extra government employees lead to bigger bureaucracies, and larger budgets. The whole plan is a colossal waste of taxpayer funds—funds that Congress could be wasting on its myriad of other insanely foolish ideas, like buying both evolution-based and creationism-based "science" books for our schools, in the interests of acknowledging all perspectives, regardless of how mindlessly ridiculous they are.

Another poorly thought-out idea that was proposed as a solution to illegal immigration was so elegantly beautiful in its simplicity that you knew there had to be a catch—the "let's just deport all them pesky illegal immigrants" plan.

Problem No. 1: There are an estimated 12 million undocumented immigrants in the continental United States.

Problem No. 2: The Immigration and Customs Enforcement [ICE] agency stated in September [2007] that the approximate cost of deporting all these people would exceed $94 billion. And in that figure, they did not completely cover the costs of hunting down and catching all those undocumented immigrants who didn't want to go back. A spokesman for the agency laid out how they arrived at that figure for CNN, and said the following:

*The undocumented worker . . . make[s] up a significant part of the economy, which would disappear if . . . illegal immigrants just fell off the face of the earth.*

"He said the amount was calculated by multiplying the estimated 12 million people by the average cost of detaining people for a day: $97. That was multiplied by the average length of detention: 32 days. ICE officials also considered transportation costs, which average $1,000 per person. But that amount can vary widely, the spokesman said. Some deportees are simply driven by bus across the border, while others must take charter planes to distant countries, he said. Finally, the department looked at personnel costs, bringing the total to roughly $94 billion."

On top of all this, one has to take into account the effect on the economy if 12 million people suddenly stopped working. The undocumented workers and their production make up a significant part of the economy, which would disappear if, as in the dreams of many politicians in both parties, illegal immigrants just fell off the face of the earth.

The economy is certainly not at its best right now, and any magical loss of illegal immigrants could, in a hypothetical scenario, crash the economy.

## The Difficulty of Immigrating Legally

But what is to be done about illegal immigration? It is certainly not fair that undocumented immigrant workers do not pay taxes, and it is certainly unfair that they use public services without contributing to it in the same way as citizens do. In order to even suggest a solution to the problem, the sources of the problem must be addressed.

Legal immigration into the United States is difficult, time consuming, and often expensive. There are complications with citizenship requirements, temporary residency, and working inside the country as a noncitizen. The citizenship examinations also, perhaps unfairly, contain technical questions about U.S. law that many American citizens cannot answer—for example, the line of presidential succession. There are few citizens who can recite the line of succession off the top of their heads beyond the president, vice president, and speaker of the house. In short, it is difficult to become a legal resident, much less a citizen, of the United States.

In the case of the most prominent source of illegal immigrants to this country, Mexico, it is particularly complicated. Public opinion is often very anti-Mexican-immigrant, and both governments are somewhat awkward in their dealings with one another on the subject of immigration itself. Mexicans are not defined as refugees by international law, even though it has become apparent in many cases that illegal immigrants are either politically or economically motivated to flee their home country.

The language doesn't help public opinion very much. The word "illegal" brings a negative response out in people, while the word "refugee" tends to bring out more empathetic feelings.

## Hypocrisy of the Hardliners

There is something deeply hypocritical about the hardliner position against illegal immigration. There seems to be contextual amnesia going on—an American citizen of the anti-immigrant persuasion can go from openly discussing the foreign origin of their ancestors to talking about how the country shouldn't [let] immigrants "come over here and steal our jobs and not speak English."

*America was built by immigrants, and that singular fact should be the first thought when it comes to dealing with the country's immigration issues.*

News flash—your ancestors were probably poor, illiterate immigrants who most of the time didn't speak English either. And they had the advantage of arriving, most likely, in an older America with much looser border controls. If you're that severely anti-immigration, you're not "conservative," and you're definitely not a "real American"—you're xenophobic [afraid of foreigners]. You're also a hypocrite. The only people who can even claim to not be descended from immigrants are Native Americans. And from what the history books say, your ancestors weren't very nice to them. The anti-immigration argument is often so flawed that it approaches the irrational.

The fact of the matter is that we should not be looking at these people with hatred and intolerance—we should be making it easier for them to become legitimate citizens, and to contribute wholly to society.

America needs all the people it can get—we certainly have the space, and with the declining birthrate, we'll need more immigrants in order to stay on par with the rising power of countries like India and China. If this country is truly ready to say no to immigrants, even the legal kind, and go to such insane lengths as to build walls and deport every undocumented person, then it might as well resign itself to becoming the next collapsed superpower. America was built by immigrants, and that singular fact should be the first thought when it comes to dealing with the country's immigration issues.

# Most Americans Do Not View Legal Immigration as a Pressing Concern

*Pew Research Center for the People & the Press*

*Pew Research Center for the People & the Press is an independent, nonpartisan public opinion research organization that studies attitudes toward politics, the press, and public policy issues.*

Most Americans do not regard immigration as a pressing concern—either for the nation or for their local community. Just 4% of all Americans volunteer immigration as the most important problem facing the country, and about the same number (3%) point to immigration as the biggest problem facing their community. Yet there are pockets of concern. In the survey of five metropolitan areas, immigration was viewed as the most serious local problem only in Phoenix. But even there, when respondents were asked in an open-ended question to identify the most important problem in the community, fewer than one-in-five (18%) volunteered immigration.

On the other hand, when asked to rate the impact of immigration among a list of five other local concerns, such as crime, traffic and the availability of jobs, 55% of Phoenix residents characterize immigration as a "very big" problem—the highest percentage for any issue—while another 23% say immigration is a "moderately big" local problem.

In Las Vegas, which like Phoenix has experienced an influx of immigrants in recent years, there also is considerable concern over immigration. More than a third of Las Vegas residents (36%) say immigration is a very big local problem, and 28% think it a moderately big problem.

However, immigration rates are less of a concern for the national public or for people living in three other American metropolitan areas with large and growing immigrant populations—Raleigh-Durham, Washington, D.C., and Chicago.

Just 21% of Americans in the national survey say immigration represents a very big problem, while 20% say it is a moderately big problem.

In Raleigh-Durham, a majority (56%) views immigration as at least a moderately big community problem, but fewer than half of Washington, D.C., residents (44%) express that opinion. For residents of the nation's capital, traffic overshadows all other local problems; fully 60% see traffic congestion as a very big problem, roughly triple the number who say that about immigration (21%), crime (20%), or education (18%).

---

*When the general public is asked its views about a comparable list of problems facing the nation, immigration ranks as a middle-tier issue.*

---

Chicago residents, in particular, express only modest concern over the effects of immigration impact on their community. Only about a third of Chicago residents (35%) see immigration as a very big or even a moderately big problem. That compares with 42% of Chicago residents who say immigration is no problem at all for their community and another 19% who view it as a small problem.

## National Immigration Concerns

When the general public is asked its views about a comparable list of problems facing the nation, immigration ranks as a middle-tier issue. Overall, 42% of the public rates immigration as a very big problem facing the nation, placing it behind the health care system (55%), terrorism (50%), crime (47%) and corrupt political leaders (46%), but a bit ahead of environmental pollution (39%) and the availability of good-paying jobs (37%).

---

*Fully twice as many conservative and moderate Democrats as liberal Democrats say immigration is a very big national problem.*

---

On a national level, immigration concerns are greatest among senior citizens, those with a high school education or less, and white evangelical Protestants. Roughly half in each of these groups rates immigration as a very big national problem.

As previous Pew surveys have shown, there are differences within both major political parties in views about the seriousness of the immigration problem. Roughly half of conservative Republicans (49%) view immigration as a very big national problem, somewhat greater than the percentage of moderate and liberal Republicans who express this view (41%). Democrats are even more divided over the seriousness of the problem presented by immigration. Fully twice as many conservative and moderate Democrats (46%) as liberal Democrats (21%) say immigration is a very big national problem.

## Legal Versus Illegal Immigration

The public overwhelmingly views illegal immigration, rather than legal immigration, as the bigger problem facing the United States. Six-in-ten Americans say illegal immigration is the bigger problem, compared with just 4% who say legal immigration. However, a sizable minority (22%) believes both illegal and legal immigration are equally worrisome. Just 11% say neither represents a big problem for the United States.

This balance of opinion is mirrored in the five metropolitan areas experiencing high levels of immigration. Solid majorities in each of the regions surveyed say illegal immigration is a bigger problem than legal immigration. And about one-in-five in each city believes that illegal and legal immigration are equally severe problems.

## Biggest Threat: Jobs, Culture, or Security?

Americans draw distinctions about the concerns they have over both legal and illegal immigration. Legal immigration is mostly seen as a threat to American jobs; 41% of those who are more worried about legal immigration (or say both forms of immigration are equal problems) say their biggest concern is that legal immigration will hurt American jobs.

By contrast, people who see illegal immigration as a bigger problem (or say both equally) are divided on their concerns. Three-in-ten (31%) say illegal immigration hurts jobs, but nearly as many (27%) say it raises the danger of terrorism, and 16% say it contributes to crime. Terrorism and crime are less frequently cited as concerns by those who say legal immigration is a bigger problem.

---

*Competition for jobs, the erosion of traditional American values, the costs to local government and the threats of terrorism and crime are all sources of concern.*

---

The idea that immigrants hurt American customs or the American way of life is a concern, though not a paramount one, of those worried about each form of immigration. About one-in-five (17%) of those more concerned about legal immigration say it is their biggest concern. Just one-in-ten (11%) of those more concerned about illegal immigration feel the same way.

## Concerns About Immigrants

Most Americans express some concern about the growing immigrant population in one way or another, but the nature of those concerns vary and are expressed with varying intensity by different segments of the population. Competition for jobs, the erosion of traditional American values, the costs to local government and the threats of terrorism and crime are all sources of immigration-related concern to some Americans, but none of these is a dominant or primary cause of worry. And on virtually every one of these points, a substantial share of the population takes a positive view of immigrants or finds no cause for concern.

For example, when asked to choose between two contrasting statements about immigrants—one which says that they represent a burden to the country because they take jobs, housing and health care; the other saying that immigrants strengthen the country through their hard work and talents—the public is divided. Just over half (52%) say that immigrants are a burden, but 41% say they strengthen the country. However, the percentage saying that immigrants are a burden is higher now than at any time since 1997. In five other surveys taken since September 2000, the share of the population expressing that view had been 44% or less.

Both whites (55%) and blacks (54%) are more likely than Hispanics (29%) to see immigrants as a burden, though attitudes are by no means uniform within any of these groups.

Views also vary according to levels of education. For example, a majority of whites with a four-year college degree (56%) say that immigrants strengthen the country through their hard work, while more than a third (37%) say that they are a burden. Whites with less than a baccalaureate education split the opposite way, with 63% seeing immigrants as burden and 30% saying that they strengthen the country. Similar, but less pronounced, differences are apparent among non-whites of differing levels of education.

Perceptions about one's personal economic situation also correlate with attitudes toward immigrants. Those who say their personal finances are only fair or poor express a negative attitude toward immigrants; 58% view them as a burden, compared with 36% who say they strengthen the country. People who rate their finances as excellent or good are divided (44% burden/48% strengthen). Religion is significant too. Among white evangelical Protestants, for example, 64% see immigrants as a burden, compared with 56% of white Catholics and 52% of white mainline Protestants. There are also differences according to political ideologies, with 58% of conservatives seeing immigrants as a burden, compared with 42% of liberals and 52% of moderates who feel this way.

People who live in areas with a high density of immigrants are evenly divided over whether immigrants strengthen the country (48%) or represent a burden (47%). By contrast, those who live where immigrants are a sparse presence voice much higher concern; 66% say they are a burden vs. 27% who believe they strengthen the country.

## Views About the Social/Economic Impact of Immigration

With respect to immigration's social impact, Americans are about evenly split between those who say the growing number of newcomers from other countries threaten traditional American customs and values (48%) and those who say that the newcomers strengthen American society (45%). The same basic differences by race, education, perceptions of economic well-being, religion and political ideology are apparent in responses to this question as for the measure of economic and fiscal concerns. And here again, the people who live in places with the sparsest immigrant populations are most likely to express concerns.

A combined total of 63% express concerns over immigration either in response to the question about threats to American values or to the question about being a burden on jobs, housing and health care. But only about four-in-ten (37%) of all respondents voiced concerns about both of these threats and burdens. This suggests that while concerns are widespread, they are not uniform—and that different people find different reasons to be concerned.

The extent of concern over immigrants' impact on jobs may be mitigated by perceptions about the kinds of work they perform. Nearly two-thirds of respondents (65%) say that immigrants mostly take jobs that Americans don't want, while a much smaller number, just 24%, say the newcomers mostly take jobs away from American citizens. Only once before in the past two decades—in 1996—have views on this question been as lopsided as they are now.

A majority of respondents in every part of the country and across all major socioeconomic, political and religious groups say that immigrants mostly take unwanted jobs. But there are some differences in the extent to which people in different groups hold this view. More Hispanics (81%) see immigrants as taking unwanted jobs than do either whites (65%) or blacks (54%). Education is also a factor. For example, among whites, 79% of those with a college education see immigrants as taking unwanted jobs, while 59% of those who do not have a baccalaureate degree hold this view.

---

*The view that most recent immigrants do not pay their fair share of taxes is shared among most segments of the population.*

---

Not surprisingly, perceptions of personal economic well-being are also an important factor in shaping these attitudes. Three-in-ten of those who say their personal finances are only fair or poor believe that immigrants take jobs from Americans, compared with 18% of those who have a positive view of their personal finances.

Americans express a mix of views about the impact of immigration on government services and budgets. A majority (56%) say that most recent immigrants do not pay their fair share of taxes, but a similarly large share (60%) say that immigrants moving into their communities have not made much of a difference in the quality of local government services.

The view that most recent immigrants do not pay their fair share of taxes is shared among most segments of the population. Education is a significant factor, particularly among whites; respondents with a four-year college education are more likely to say immigrants pay their fair share than are those with less education.

Most Americans (60%) say that the immigrants moving into their communities in recent years have not made much of a difference in the quality of their local government services, while about a quarter (26%) say that immigrants have made those services worse and 7% say they have made them better. With only small variations, this same basic judgment about the impact of immigration on local government services is expressed by all segments of the population.

# CHAPTER 2

# Are Illegal Immigrants Treated Fairly?

# Chapter Preface

On May 1, 2009, immigrant workers staged marches across America to highlight the importance of immigrant labor to the U.S. economy and to demand rights for the estimated 12 million illegal immigrants—sometimes called undocumented workers—currently residing in the country. The 2009 marches were a repeat of May Day marches held each year since 2006, when thousands of immigrants and their supporters first filled the streets of major U.S. cities. Although the 2009 marches were much smaller than in previous years, perhaps because of the slowdown in the U.S. economy, marchers continued to send the same message employed in earlier protests—that foreigners come to the United States to work, not to break laws, and that they should be treated with respect rather than as criminals. Immigrant supporters seek compassion and support for all immigrants, and they hope to convince policy makers to change the nation's immigration laws to provide what they characterize as more humane treatment for immigrants.

Immigrants' rights supporters maintain that illegal immigration serves a valuable purpose for the U.S. economy—providing cheap and compliant labor for U.S. employers. Yet these employers benefit at the workers' expense; the illegal status of these workers makes them vulnerable to unscrupulous employers, who may deny them minimum wages or overtime pay, or fire workers who dare to protest working conditions or attempt to join unions. At the same time, it is the workers, not the employers, who are usually the target of immigration enforcement efforts. The George W. Bush administration, for example, carried out a number of high-profile workplace raids and deported thousands of illegal immigrant workers in recent years. In some cases, these raids uprooted individuals who had lived in the United States for many years, along with their families. Fear of deportation, advocates argue, forces illegal immigrants in the country to live in the shadows of American life—a situation that they contend is hypocritical and contrary to American values. The immigrants' rights movement compares itself to the civil rights movement of the 1960s, when black Americans fought for greater civil rights.

Specifically, immigrants' rights supporters oppose what they view as punitive immigration policies that make it a crime for U.S. employers to hire illegal immigrants and that allow the federal government to carry out workplace raids and deportations of workers who have entered or stayed in the United States without proper immigration papers. They also object to systems, such as E-Verify, set up by the federal government to allow employers to check the immigration status of each worker. Immigrant advocates claim that such systems are often inaccurate and cause employers to discriminate against all Hispanics, even those who may be U.S. citizens or legal visa holders. Finally, immigrants' rights supporters oppose any type of guest worker program—which would allow large employers to recruit temporary laborers—because they think it would deny workers basic rights and social equality. Advocates want U.S. immigration policies to be reformed to end all workplace raids and deportations, to increase the number of legal visas available to foreign workers, and to offer amnesty and a path to citizenship to all 12 million illegal immigrants currently residing in the United States.

Many observers, however, are outraged at the sight of immigrants demanding rights in a country where they cannot even claim legal status. Those on this side of the issue believe that every country, including the United States, has a right to control immigration numbers, and they see illegal immigrants as lawbreakers who should not benefit from their unlawful behavior. These commentators typically oppose amnesty or other programs that would provide legal status, citizenship, or other rights or benefits to resident illegal immigrants. Many anti-immigration advocates also would like to reduce the levels of illegal immigration, through better border security and stronger enforcement of existing laws—to deport illegal workers and prevent employers from hiring immigrants who lack legal visas.

Immigrants' rights supporters often dismiss these contrary views as racist in motivation, or simply lacking in empathy. Clearly, the demands for amnesty and immigrant rights do raise difficult questions about whether the United States treats illegal immigrants fairly and how the country can enforce immigration laws more humanely. The authors of the viewpoints in this chapter present some examples of the two sides of this highly polarized issue.

# Illegal Immigrants Are Often Treated More Fairly than U.S. Citizens

*Arlene Jones*

*Arlene Jones is a resident of Chicago and a featured columnist for the* Austin Weekly News, *the top weekly newspaper serving the Austin neighborhood of Chicago.*

This Friday, May 1, [2009] will again bring about marches from people who are in this country illegally and their supporters. Illegal immigration is a very contentious subject. This year it will be even more so as millions of Americans have become unemployed or are facing the "chopping block."

## Where Is the Fairness?

I always have been insulted when individuals who are pro-illegal immigrants try to logic out why one group of people can break one set of laws while the rest of us should be subject to the exact same laws. For example, the city of Chicago has proclaimed itself to be a sanctuary city. We have individuals who get upset if the police do stings and arrest and take the cars of people who are in this country illegally and driving without a license. Yet we recently had an alderman proclaim that the city should take the cars of American citizens who leave traffic court and drive after being told to not do so. Where is the fairness?

I recently spent several months working in a Chicago public school where the student population was half black and half Hispanic. As I walked down the hallways, the classrooms for grades kindergarten through third looked like something out of a movie prior to *Brown vs. Board of Education* [1954

Supreme Court ruling that outlawed racial segregation in public schools]. The classrooms for first graders, for example, had all the black children in one room while all the Hispanic children were in a separate classroom.

---

*If the Hispanic children are getting bilingual education, shouldn't the black kids be getting the same opportunity to become bilingual . . . ?*

---

Why? Because six years prior, two children were born in the same city and same hospital. The black child went home where he/she learned English even if it was the Ebonics [a dialect of standard American English spoken by some African Americans] version. The other child went home with parents who didn't speak English and may be in this country illegally. That child learned Spanish as their first language.

When the time came to go to school, the Hispanic parents were allowed to choose a bilingual education program, even if the child is functional in English.

Wait a second. If the Hispanic children are getting bilingual education, shouldn't the black kids be getting the same opportunity to become bilingual by learning Spanish at the same time the Hispanic children are learning English? Where is the fairness?

Recently, a man testified before Congress regarding his daughter who was killed while sitting in her car at a red light. Her car was hit by a drunk driver, who was an illegal immigrant. The father referred to the people listed on the ICE [Immigration and Customs Enforcement] database of illegal immigrants with criminal backgrounds as "banditos." The father was subsequently chastised by Congressman Luis Gutierrez for using the term "banditos." Interestingly enough, it was not because the congressman could point to the term as being derogatory, but because he has chosen to pursue the interest of illegal immigrants over those of U.S. citizens. He was more concerned with how the illegal immigrants were being portrayed than he was about a U.S. citizen being killed by someone who shouldn't have been in the country to begin with. Where is the fairness?

---

*As Americans have lost jobs, houses and their version of the American dream, will we as a country still be gullible enough to believe that there are jobs that we won't do?*

---

I have watched while a friend of mine lost his restaurant business. Every day he was visited by the city and issued fines for violations that had nothing to do with his food handling. Fines for signage violation. Fines because his video game didn't have a current license even though it was unplugged and facing backwards so that no one could use it. Yet, every day on the streets of Austin, I am seeing unlicensed and unsanitary corn carts sitting on corners vending food. There is no running water to wash hands and, even worse, where do they use the bathroom when they stand on a corner for hours on end?

I saw on North Avenue, by the soon-to-be opened new Menards, a man cooking tacos on the city's sidewalk. I am sure we have tons of Americans who could also put a BBQ pit on a cart and stand on a corner and sell food. Yet it doesn't happen because the city enforces food handling laws against citizens but not against others. Where is the fairness?

As this year's marches occur, I am anxious to see how illegal immigration will be portrayed. As Americans have lost jobs, houses and their version of the American dream, will we as a country still be gullible enough to believe that there are jobs that we won't do?

# Illegal Immigrants Have No Right to Be Treated as Equals to Citizens

*Dennis Byrne*

*Dennis Byrne is a Chicago-based writer and consultant.*

As the Senate is entering the great debate over illegal immigration [2006], it's imperative to examine the frequent claim of "immigrants' rights."

Bluntly said, people who are illegally in this country possess only those civil rights that we grant to them.

Yes, they have human rights, such as the familiar life, liberty and the pursuit of happiness. But civil rights, by most definitions, are protections and privileges of freedom given by nation's laws to its citizens.

This, of course, flies in the face of the contemporary confusion about "immigrants' rights," which proclaim that anyone who lands on U.S. soil, by whatever means, has the same civil right to obtain a driver's license, get a subsidized mortgage or any of the other benefits that are typically granted by law to citizens.

---

*If the citizens of the United States don't get to decide who qualifies for citizenship and who benefits from government programs, then citizenship is made meaningless.*

---

An illegal immigrant can claim the protections of human rights, which cannot be voided by any governmental action. But—and this will startle and anger some—an "undocumented" immigrant has no claim to equal treatment.

Dennis Byrne, "When Illegal Means Illegal," RealClearPolitics.com, March 7, 2006. www.realclearpolitics.com. Reproduced by permission.

## Real Implications

This may sound like a lot of philosophical gibberish, but it has some very real implications. For example, the teen who was in America illegally and who was denied admission to an Elmwood Park [Illinois] school has a human right to an education. But whether she has a civil right to attend that school, using our public money, at this time, should be a matter for the citizens of the United States and Elmwood Park to decide. Same goes for issuing driver's licenses or providing mortgage assistance.

I might sound like a squirrely policy wonk for saying it, but if the citizens of the United States don't get to decide who qualifies for citizenship and who benefits from government programs, then citizenship is made meaningless by denying them control over their laws and their spending. So, Americans are properly offended by the bald-faced attempt by Mexican president Vicente Fox and 10 other Latin American leaders to prescribe their solution to the vast problems caused by the illegal presence of 11 million people in our country and a nonfunctional border.

---

*In 1986, we conducted this same debate and the "solution" then was to grant amnesty to about 2.7 million illegal immigrants.*

---

While we're trying to set some ground rules in this difficult debate, it would help to clarify some language. A foreigner (yes, that's the proper name for someone here from another country) who can't produce his documents to demonstrate his legal status in the United States is different from a foreigner who has no documents because he is here illegally. Thus, "undocumented immigrant" is an imprecise substitute for "illegal immigrant."

It is yet another loss for proper usage in the never-ending skirmish over political correctness. And while the use of "illegal immigrant" may cause offense, it hardly rises to the offensive heights caused by labeling one side of a legitimate debate "nativists" or "xenophobes."

## Learning from the Past

Also, as we enter this debate, it's wise to bring up what we've learned from the past, since we've been around this corner before. In 1986, we conducted this same debate and the "solution" then was to grant amnesty to about 2.7 million illegal immigrants. Then, amnesty advocates said we need grant it "just this once," and that better enforcement—mostly going after employers who hire illegal immigrants—would solve the problem. That amnesty didn't stop the illegal flow across our border, and enforcement—especially by the [George W.] Bush administration—has been a joke.

Last year [2005], 86 members of Congress felt compelled to urge President Bush to enforce three dozen immigration laws that they said the administration had ignored.

Amnesty wasn't part of a border-security bill the House passed last year. But the Senate won't escape a debate over amnesty, especially with President Bush pushing for a "guest worker" program. At least four bills are up for Senate consideration, but as far as I can tell, none of them would immediately round up 11 million people and ship them "back." Nonetheless, some believe any solution is so intractable that we might as well live with an open border.

To the contrary, we can solve this problem, humanely and effectively. Strengthen our border. Enforce the laws on the books. Restore respect for the rule of law. Agree that the fight isn't over immigration, but illegal immigration. And, most important, agree that Americans have a right to define and defend what it means to be an American.

# Illegal Immigrant Workers Can Be Exploited

*Jesse Walker*

*Managing editor of* Reason *magazine, Jesse Walker is also the author of* Rebels on the Air: An Alternative History of Radio in America.

In April, Tzu Ming Yang and Jack Chang of Clarksville, a wealthy Baltimore suburb, pleaded guilty to charges of conspiracy to harbor illegal aliens and launder money. Yang's wife, Jui Fan Lee Yang, copped to employing the illegals at Kawasaki, the trio's Baltimore sushi chain. The conspiracy charges could lead to sentences of up to 30 years in prison, and Chang and the Yangs will have to forfeit more than $1 million in property.

The case was noted far beyond the boundaries of Baltimore. The *Washington Post* called it a sign that "serious criminal charges once typically reserved for drug traffickers and organized crime figures are increasingly being used to target businesses that employ illegal immigrants." That's one important angle to the story. Just as interesting, though, is what the case tells us about the bizarre double bind our immigration laws create for alien workers.

## Exploitation of Illegal Immigrants

According to the affidavit of Brian Smeltzer, a special agent with U.S. Immigration and Customs Enforcement, the investigation began with an anonymous letter claiming Kawasaki "paid the illegal aliens low wages, no overtime, and took their tips; in return, Tzu Yang promised to file paperwork for the illegal aliens to obtain work visas." (Smeltzer does not say whether Yang followed through on his promise.) An attachment to Mrs. Yang's plea explained that the restaurants required the employees "to work more than forty hours a week and paid them in cash amounts substantially less than required by law." Perhaps three-quarters of the employees were here illegally, housed by their employers in dirty, cramped conditions.

The bosses, meanwhile, spent their profits on luxury cars, which the affidavit lists in exhaustive detail. They come off as capitalist villains straight out of central casting; you'd have to arrest Ebenezer Scrooge and C. Montgomery Burns to find such unattractive defendants.

## The Double Bind

Yet immigrant rights groups aren't very enthusiastic about this sort of work site enforcement. It's not hard to see why: Liberated from their taskmasters, the illegal aliens are being deported. Two have already been sent home to El Salvador, while 13 others, Asian natives all, are "on electronic monitoring pending their removal," according to Marcia Murphy, a public affairs specialist at the U.S. Attorney's Office in Baltimore.

There's a whole genre of free market literature that defends sweatshops and the like on the grounds that they're the best available option for their workers—jobs they've freely chosen because the immediate alternatives are all worse. I don't reject that argument outright, but I've never found it entirely satisfying either. That's partly because some of those sweatshop titans don't just give their charges low wages and long hours; they engage in coercion or fraud. It's one thing to choose a job because the alternatives look worse. It's quite another to find yourself cheated out of your pay at the end of the day or, worse, held captive on a citrus farm with hundreds of other workers and threatened with death if you try to leave.

(The latter scenario is a real case in south Florida, where employers Ramiro, Juan, and José Ramos were convicted in 2002 of extortion and slavery.)

But there's another problem with the argument, a factor that's in play even with enterprises that deal with their workers honestly and nonviolently. Yes, sometimes what look like lousy conditions to us are the best option an employee has, and if you shut down their workplace they'll be even worse off. But sometimes the only reason those conditions are the least bad choice available is because the other possibilities have been cut off by legal fiat.

---

*If they were treated as poorly as the government says they were, then those workers certainly deserve a chance to be free . . .*

---

## Little Recourse for Defrauded Illegal Immigrants

I'm referring not just to illegal immigrants, who for obvious reasons have little recourse if they're defrauded or enslaved, but to guest workers, who come here under strict rules that prevent them from changing jobs, let alone striking out on their own. This isn't free labor operating in an open marketplace. It's a work force whose power and mobility have been limited by law.

There's no excuse for stealing from your workers or for forcibly keeping them on the job. But crackdowns on abusive employers will bring little justice if the result for their victims is a one-way ticket home. I ate at the Charles Street Kawasaki two or three times myself, before the immigration gendarmes rolled in, and I remember that the workers were friendly, helpful people. I even recall tipping a bit more than usual, not realizing my money would end up in someone else's pocket. If they were treated as poorly as the government says they were, then those workers certainly deserve a chance to be free of Kawasaki's clutches. Not to be sent back to Asia or Latin America, but to find a better job, openly and legally, at the Italian restaurant across the street.

# The Increased Use of Detention as Part of U.S. Immigration Enforcement Violates Human Rights

*Amnesty International*

*Amnesty International is an international human rights organization.*

Migration is a fact of life. Some people move to new countries to improve their economic situation or to pursue their education. Others leave their countries to escape armed conflict or violations of their human rights, such as torture, persecution, or extreme poverty. Many move for a combination of reasons. Governments have the right to exercise authority over their borders; however, they also have obligations under international law to protect the human rights of migrants, no matter what prompted an individual to leave his or her home country. . . .

## Detention Violates Human Rights

In just over a decade, immigration detention has tripled. In 1996, immigration authorities had a daily detention capacity of less than 10,000. Today more than 30,000 immigrants are detained each day, and this number is likely to increase even further in 2009.

More than 300,000 men, women and children are detained by US immigration authorities each year. They include asylum seekers, torture survivors, victims of human trafficking, long-time lawful permanent residents, and the parents of US citizen children. The use of detention as a tool to combat unau-

Amnesty International, *Jailed Without Justice: Immigration Detention in the USA*. New York: Amnesty International, 2009. Reproduced by permission.

thorized migration falls short of international human rights law, which contains a clear presumption against detention. Everyone has the right to liberty, freedom of movement, and the right not to be arbitrarily detained.

---

*Approximately 1.8 million people migrate to the United States every year.*

---

The dramatic increase in the use of immigration detention has forced US immigration authorities to contract with approximately 350 state and county criminal jails across the country to house individuals pending deportation proceedings. Approximately 67 percent of immigration detainees are held in these facilities, while the remaining individuals are held in facilities operated by immigration authorities and private contractors. The average cost of detaining a migrant is $95 per person, per day. Alternatives to detention, which generally involve some form of reporting, are significantly cheaper, with some programs costing as little as $12 per day. These alternatives to detention have been shown to be effective with an estimated 91 percent appearance rate before the immigration courts. Despite the effectiveness of these less expensive and less restrictive alternatives to detention in ensuring compliance with immigration procedures, the use of immigration detention continues to rise at the expense of the United States' human rights obligations.

## Unauthorized Immigrants in the United States

Approximately 1.8 million people migrate to the United States every year. The vast majority have official authorization to live and work in the United States. Less than a quarter do not have permission to enter the United States, and they live and work in the country as unauthorized immigrants. The US government estimates that as of January 2007, there were almost 12 million unauthorized immigrants living in the United States. They come from countries around the world—the top five countries of origin are Mexico, El Salvador, Guatemala, the Philippines, and China. Unauthorized immigrants often live in the shadows and are at heightened risk of exploitation, discrimination and abuse. They often work in degrading conditions and are frequently denied access to many forms of health care, housing, and other services. Individuals committing abuses against immigrants know that they are unlikely to be held accountable, because unauthorized immigrants are often reluctant to turn to the authorities, fearing the possibility of arrest or deportation.

---

*Entering or remaining in the United States without authorization is a civil violation, not a crime.*

---

Politicians, public officials, and the media have a significant impact on the public's perception of immigrants and their rights. Much of the public debate about immigration in the United States, particularly in the wake of the attacks of September 11 [2001], is framed around issues of national security and the economy. One prime-time host of a national news channel stated, "Illegal aliens . . . not only threaten our economy and security, but also our health and well-being. . . ." Such comments contribute to a climate of fear and create the impression that immigrants do not—and should not—have any rights at all.

## Immigration Enforcement Policies

Entering or remaining in the United States without authorization is a civil violation, not a crime. The Department of Homeland Security (DHS) has broad discretion to apprehend individuals it suspects of immigration violations. Individuals may be apprehended at the border, during employment or household raids, as a result of traffic stops by local police, or after having been convicted of a criminal offense.

There are two divisions within DHS tasked with immigration enforcement: Customs and Border Protection (CBP) is responsible for enforcement at the border, and Immigration and Customs Enforcement (ICE) is responsible for enforcement within the United States. If DHS has a reasonable belief that an individual does not have permission to enter or remain in the United States, then that person may be placed in "removal proceedings," which means the government is seeking to deport him or her from the United States.

---

*Amnesty International found that immigrants . . . may be detained for months or even years as they go through deportation procedures.*

---

Individuals apprehended by immigration authorities often do not know what is happening and may not understand what their rights are. Many may accept immediate deportation even though they may not have had an opportunity to consult with an attorney and they may not actually be deportable. A person may be eligible to remain in the United States for a variety of reasons, including a well-founded fear of persecution in his or her home country, having a US citizen spouse, or exceptional hardship caused to his or her US citizen children. Amnesty International has identified more than a hundred cases in the past ten years in which US citizens and lawful permanent residents have incorrectly been placed into removal proceedings.

## Rights During Deportations

Individuals subject to deportation still have human rights. International law requires that deportation procedures follow due process and conform to international human rights standards. Like any other circumstance, detention pending removal proceedings must be justified as a necessary and proportionate measure in each individual case, and should only be used as a measure of last resort and be subject to judicial review.

While ICE reported an average detention stay of 37 days in 2007, Amnesty International found that immigrants and asylum seekers may be detained for months or even years as they go through deportation procedures that will determine whether or not they are eligible to remain in the United States.

For example, according to a 2003 study, asylum seekers who were eventually granted asylum spent an average of 10 months in detention with the longest reported period being 3.5 years. Amnesty International has documented several cases, detailed in this report, in which individuals have been detained for four years. Individuals who have been ordered deported may languish in detention indefinitely if their home country is unwilling to accept their return or does not have diplomatic relations with the United States.

An important safeguard against arbitrary detention is the ability of an individual to challenge his or her detention before an independent judicial body. The US criminal justice system provides individuals detained and charged with criminal offenses with the opportunity to challenge their detention before a court and provides legal counsel for individuals who cannot afford to pay themselves. However, individuals detained on the basis of civil immigration violations are not provided with such safeguards. Many individuals are held in immigration detention without access to an immigration judge or judicial body and have to represent themselves if they cannot afford a lawyer. Factors such as whether an individual is apprehended at the border, whether an individual is apprehended within the United States, and whether an individual has been convicted of certain crimes may determine whether that individual is detained and what kind of review, if any, takes place.

In the case of individuals who are apprehended at the border, an immigration officer makes decisions about whether or not the person will remain in detention—these individuals are not entitled to a review of their detention by an immigration judge. Those apprehended inside the United States are entitled to a review by an immigration judge. However, this review does not always take place, or does not take place in a timely manner.

Individuals who have lived in the United States for years can be subject to "mandatory detention," meaning there is no opportunity for an individual hearing to determine whether he or she should be released, and deported for minor crimes they committed years ago. Thousands of individuals every year are subject to mandatory detention while deportation proceedings take place. It is not known exactly how many individuals are subject to mandatory detention, and DHS did not respond to a request from Amnesty International to provide this data. US citizens and lawful permanent residents have been incorrectly subject to mandatory detention, and have spent months or years behind bars before being able to prove they are not deportable from the United States.

*There is an urgent need to ensure that all facilities housing immigration detainees comply with international human rights law and standards.*

The ability to access the outside world is an essential safeguard against arbitrary detention. However, Amnesty International documented significant barriers immigrants face in accessing assistance and support while in detention. Problems included lack of access to legal counsel and consulates; lack of access to law libraries along with inadequate access to telephones; and frequent and sudden transfers of detainees to facilities located far away from courts, advocates, and family.

Amnesty International also documented pervasive problems with conditions of detention, such as commingling of immigration detainees with individuals convicted of criminal offenses; inappropriate and excessive use of restraints; inadequate access to health care, including mental health services; and inadequate access to exercise. In 2000, immigration authorities introduced detailed detention standards for facilities housing immigration detainees, covering issues such as access to attorneys and conditions of detention. However, these guidelines are not binding regulations and are not legally enforceable.

## Improving Conditions

In September 2008, ICE announced the publication of 41 new performance-based detention standards, which are to be implemented over 18 months and will take full effect in all facilities housing ICE detainees by January 2010. Amnesty International welcomes this step toward improving conditions in immigration detention; however these are still only guidelines and are not legally enforceable. Amnesty International findings indicate that conditions of detention in many facilities do not meet either international human rights standards or ICE guidelines. There is an urgent need to ensure that all facilities housing immigration detainees comply with international human rights law and standards. Ensuring that detention standards are legally binding, and creating a mechanism for independent oversight of their implementation, would better protect the human rights of immigrants in detention in the United States.

CHAPTER 3

# How Should the U.S. Government Respond to Illegal Immigration?

# Chapter Preface

In response to calls for increased security on the border between the United States and Mexico, the U.S. Department of Homeland Security (DHS) in 2005 announced the Secure Border Initiative (SBI)—a comprehensive, nine-year plan to secure U.S. borders and reduce illegal immigration. The plan includes adding more border patrol agents, securing ports of entry, expanding detention facilities, constructing more border fences, increasing enforcement of immigration laws, and implementing various technology upgrades, such as a "virtual fence." The first part of the effort—adding agents and building more physical fences and infrastructure—has largely been completed. In May 2009, DHS began the high-tech part of the SBI project—a $6.7 billion surveillance system utilizing cameras, sensors, and other technology designed to eventually cover almost all of the two thousand-mile U.S.-Mexican border.

The idea behind the SBI plan is to integrate three components—people, fences, and technology—to establish more effective control of the U.S. southern border. In some high-traffic areas, modern physical fences and a concentration of border patrol agents may be the most effective system for securing the border. More remote areas, on the other hand, may be better controlled by high-tech surveillance devices that take the place of physical fences and border patrols. These devices are designed to alert personnel when human activity is detected. An environmental plus is that wildlife would still be allowed to have unrestricted movement across the border in areas monitored electronically.

The first part of the virtual fence surveillance system, called SBInet, will cover a twenty-three-mile stretch of the border south of Tucson, Arizona. The system will employ nine surveillance towers, which will stand one hundred and forty feet and will be equipped with a networked system of radars, ground and air sensors, and day/night cameras to monitor the border. There will also be a series of control stations built to receive and process information. If the system detects activity, U.S. agents can be dispatched to the areas to pick up border crossers before they are able to melt into the U.S. population.

The contract for the Arizona portion of SBInet was awarded to Boeing in September 2006, with the expectation that it would be up and running by the end of 2008. The program ran into significant problems, however, and a twenty-eight-mile test portion was widely viewed as a failure. The project encountered software glitches; the sensitive equipment was not able to stand up to Arizona heat and weather; camera images were sometimes fuzzy; and radar systems had difficulty distinguishing humans from animals and sagebrush, and were sometimes triggered by rain. The current project will replace much of that earlier, failed prototype. The hope now is that the first phase in Tucson, Arizona, will be operational by the fall of 2009, and all of Arizona by 2011.

If the Arizona portion of the virtual fence is successful, DHS will add the surveillance system to other parts of the southern border. The next state slated to receive funding is New Mexico, then California, and finally Texas. The early problems with SBInet, however, have caused some in U.S. Congress to question whether the very idea of a virtual fence is viable. Some border experts are also skeptical of the cost and benefits of SBInet. Representatives of the National Border Patrol Council (NBPC), an organization that represents more than 12,000 border patrol agents, has argued that the technology only works on level ground. In areas where the terrain is more mountainous—with boulders, vegetation, and valleys— the surveillance system has much more difficulty. The only solution would be to add more towers in those areas, an idea that would be too costly for such a long border. Many critics, in fact, see the virtual fence as a very expensive boondoggle that should not be awarded any more public funding.

Border control, however, is only one of many ideas for how the United States should respond to illegal immigration. The authors of the viewpoints in this chapter discuss several other proposals, many of them variations on the two most controversial themes: granting amnesty to illegal immigrants already in the country and stepping up immigration enforcement efforts.

# The United States Should Adopt a More Humane Border Policy

*Border Network for Human Rights, Border Action Network, and U.S.-Mexico Border and Immigration Task Force*

*The Border Network for Human Rights, Border Action Network, and the U.S.-Mexico Border and Immigration Task Force are nongovernmental groups in the Southwest United States, formed to promote effective border and immigration policies.*

For too many years, we have witnessed efforts to secure the border that are grounded not in the complex realities of border life but in simplistic sound bites and assumptions that building a wall can somehow keep our country safe. Our conclusions and policy recommendations start with the premise that the "border" is a dynamic concept, that border communities have important ties to both the United States and Mexico, and that these ties create a unique set of opportunities and challenges that affect both the border areas and the broader national interest. Recognizing that millions live and work in U.S. border communities, border and immigration policies must be formulated and implemented in a way that respects the rights of these community members and the needs of their hometowns and cities. When properly carried out, these policies can substantially improve security and safety in the border region and in the nation as a whole.

## The Consequences of Increased Militarization of the Border

Over the last two decades, U.S. immigration policy began to focus increasingly on the need to secure the southwest border in order to block the flow of undocumented migrants. Rather

*U.S.-Mexico Border Policy Report.* El Paso, TX: Border Network for Human Rights, Border Action Network, and U.S.-Mexico Border and Immigration Task Force, 2008. Reproduced by permission.

than viewing border enforcement as a component of a broader immigration strategy, border enforcement became the strategy, most often expressed as the need to first secure our borders before dealing with broader questions of immigration reform. This approach, however, has failed, costing the country billions of dollars, weakening the autonomy and rights of border communities and their residents, and creating a militarized border that has left the country less secure. Our findings indicate that the consequences of these policies have led to needless suffering and an overall degradation in human rights.

*By ensuring the safety of border communities, we shift away from an enforcement-only mentality to one that recognizes that smart immigration reforms benefit everyone.*

## Recommendations

The U.S.-Mexico Border and Immigration Task Force has developed over 70 specific recommendations for improving immigration enforcement. The vast majority of the recommendations identify specific ways to improve enforcement objectives, reduce the possibility of civil and human rights violations, and engage border communities in creating solutions to legitimate concerns about violence and security along the border, as well as for calling for an end to misguided and fiscally irresponsible programs, such as the mandatory construction of a physical border wall. Some of these suggestions have already been recognized by Congress and incorporated into proposals such as the STRIVE Act of 2007 and the bipartisan Senate immigration proposal of 2007, including the creations of the U.S.-Mexico Border [Enforcement] Review Commission, the Congressional report on border deaths, the Border Patrol Training [Capacity] Review, local community consultations, and the Office of Detention Oversight. We believe these recommendations can and should be part of any new discussions on legislative reform of border safety.

Our recommendations offer the country an opportunity to revisit the discussions of border enforcement and immigration enforcement more generally. The ability of elected officials, law enforcement officials, business leaders, community advocates and faith leaders to come together around these proposals demonstrates that broad support can exist for immigration reform and border security, and that people from very different perspectives can agree when we challenge our assumptions. The Border [and Immigration] Task Force began to learn that much of our work centers on the question of what genuinely makes our communities safer and stronger. Thus, we believe that the report offers a new paradigm for immigration enforcement. By ensuring the safety of border communities, we shift away from an enforcement-only mentality to one that recognizes that smart immigration reforms benefit everyone in our communities and in our nation. The following summary of recommendations reflects that conclusion.

- *Communities are more secure when border enforcement policies focus on the criminal element and engage immigrants in fighting the real dangers facing us.* Community security is an integral part of national and border security, but we need to stop treating the immigrant as the greatest threat, focusing instead on dangerous criminals, traffickers, and exploiters in border and immigrant communities.

- *Communities are safer when we implement policies that ensure accountability and provide local oversight of enforcement activities.* Border enforcement policies, projects, and agencies need to be accountable to the communities in which they operate. To ensure that this occurs, the U.S. Congress needs to create an independent oversight and review commission. Additional operational and policy recommendations include improved human rights training of officers, strengthened complaint procedures, and measures to end racial profiling in the borderlands.

- *Communities flourish when ports of entry are treated as vital gateways to America.* Ports of entry are America's gateway. They are vital to the economy and well-being of the nation and border region, and they deserve major investments in staffing and infrastructure to expedite crossings and reduce the economic impact of long border delays. Dramatic overhaul of complaint and oversight procedures is needed to ensure that the rights of border crossers are protected.

- *Communities are stronger and lives are saved when we replace border blockade operations with more sensible enforcement.* Comprehensive immigration reform will eliminate the need for mass border enforcement "operations" that are responsible for hundreds of deaths annually. Implementation of border enforcement actions, technologies, and infrastructure need to take into account impacted communities and the environment.

- *Communities are literally divided by the devastating impact of the border wall, the construction of which should be halted.* The construction of the border wall should immediately stop due to its overwhelming social, environmental, and legal impacts. Just from a cost-effectiveness standpoint, the current border wall and fencing projects have not proven successful in stopping immigration flows, while construction costs have nearly doubled from $4.5 million per mile to $7.5 million per mile.

- *Communities are safer when local law enforcement is not pressed into immigration-enforcement roles.* Federal immigration laws involve complicated administrative and criminal issues, and local law-enforcement agencies should not be forced to assume the role of federal immigration enforcement. Federal and state laws and resources should not be used to pressure local agencies to undertake these activities.

- *Communities are safer when the military is not used to enforce civilian law.* The military does not belong in civilian law enforcement, even indirectly. Demonstrated risks to civilians of military operations in support of civilian law enforcement should be eliminated. Loopholes in the Posse Comitatus Act governing the National Guard should be closed.

- *Communities are destabilized by harsh detention and removal practices. It is essential to dramatically overhaul detention practices and the manner in which we conduct removals.* We propose a series of specific reforms to improve the human rights conditions of the U.S. detention and deportation system, which currently has little oversight and accountability.

---

*Our economic crisis makes it imperative that we revisit old ideas about immigration as a barrier and instead view immigration and border issues as part of the solution.*

---

- *All communities benefit by engaging the root causes of migratory pressures. Comprehensive economic development is the long-term solution.* Just and comprehensive development in the U.S. borderlands, the U.S. interior, and the Mexican interior, is the long-term solution to migratory pressures.

## Going Forward

Resolving the crisis along our southwestern border is a national imperative. The expertise of border leadership is critical to the development of border security measures. For too long, border communities have been told what will "work" to fix the problem, without being actively included in the decision-making process. At the onset of a new administration and a new Congress, the time has come to engage in a genuine dialogue about immigration and border reform. The timing could not be more critical—our economic crisis makes it imperative that we revisit old ideas about immigration as a barrier and instead view immigration and border issues as part of the solution. Effective border policy relies on:

- Security that focuses on criminal elements such as trafficking, smuggling and other insidious actions.

- Accountability and trust between law enforcement officials and the community.

- Fiscally responsible border enforcement measures that promote cross-border trade.

Ultimately, this border policy report can provide us with the opportunity to begin to address the very complicated issues of immigration reform and border security in a new framework, one that recognizes that we must all work together to remain strong and grow.

# The Government Should Rethink the Idea of Granting Amnesty to Illegal Immigrants

*Bradley Vasoli*

*Bradley Vasoli is a reporter for the* Bulletin, *a Philadelphia newspaper.*

W hile much of the immigration debate has long concerned how to fill "jobs that Americans won't do," a report examining one instance of immigration enforcement takes issue with that premise.

## Immigrant Versus American Jobs

Jerry Kammer, a senior research fellow at the Washington, D.C.-based Center for Immigration Studies (CIS), wrote a backgrounder released yesterday [March 18, 2009] that examines the impact of immigration enforcement on six meat processing plants owned by Swift & Co. As a result of heightened screening and a major December 2006 workplace raid, plants in Iowa, Minnesota, Nebraska, Texas, Colorado and Utah lost an estimated 3,000 illegal immigrant workers to firings and arrests.

How did the plants cope? Each of the six facilities took between four and five months to restart full production. But after that point, Swift was reportedly able to staff its four beef plants and two pork plants with native-born and legal immigrant workers.

Swift could do so, Mr. Kammer wrote, in part because of the signing bonuses and wage hikes it adopted for at least four of the plants after 2006. These new policies amounted on average to a 7.7-percent increase in earnings for those plants' production workers.

Mr. Kammer said the relevant data shows whether or not a job is one Americans will do partly depends on how lucrative that job is. That, he added, often doesn't remain static.

"It's just that certain jobs are defined as 'immigrant jobs' over time," he said.

## Another View

Other immigration experts take a different view of the success of the Swift plants in reconstructing its production staffs with native-born Americans and other legal residents.

Tamar Jacoby, president of ImmigrationWorks USA, said some reporting on the Swift plants suggests while they saw an upsurge in domestic workers in the short term, they had difficulty retaining many of those workers because of the arduous working conditions.

---

*President Barack Obama and Congress should rethink their hope to [grant] amnesty [to] the vast majority of illegal aliens currently residing in the United States.*

---

Ms. Jacoby said companies that are forced to raise wages too rapidly sometimes face difficulty continuing their operations in the United States because they end up passing the increased costs onto their consumers, thereby making their products less competitive.

"There's only so high they can go and remain competitive with global products," she said, adding she did believe wages must meet a reasonable living standard. "I'm not defending below-market wages or indecent wages, but I am saying there is a limit to how much employers in certain industries can raise the wages and still remain competitive."

United States Department of Agriculture [USDA] statistics cited in the CIS study showed, in the case of meat products, wages and benefits for production workers account for between 7 and 9 percent of consumer prices. Hence, according to those figures, if pay and benefits to those workers went up by a third, retail prices would go up by a maximum of 3 percent.

## Policy Implications

A major policy implication of the study, Mr. Kammer said, is that President Barack Obama and Congress should rethink their hope to [grant] amnesty [to] the vast majority of illegal aliens currently residing in the United States. Such a policy was tried before in 1986 and, he said, that has only swelled the influx of illegals because immigrants in the United States spread the word about the generosity of America's immigration policy to relatives back home.

"Instead of amnesty controlling it or containing it, it led to a vast expansion of it," he said. "The immigration networks work with great efficiency."

# Illegal Immigrants Should Be Offered Second-Class Citizenship

*Michael Vass*

*Michael Vass is a businessman, president of MV Consulting, and author of Black Entertainment USA, a Web blog about how African American and Hispanic entertainers are portrayed in the media.*

From time to time I have discussed the question of immigration in America. To be direct, I do not like any illegal immigrant being in the nation, and absolutely believe that they deserve nothing from the government if they are here. That being said, if you want to give up your home for immigrants to stay at and your income for them to live reading further will only anger you.

## No Rights for Noncitizens

Again I will start with a clarification. They are not undocumented workers. That is polispeak [quotes by politicians] for illegal alien or more accurately illegal immigrant. The document they are missing is a green card—which would give them legal purpose to be in this nation. Thus every single illegal alien is a willful criminal first and foremost.

---

*I have no problem with my taxes going to help those in need, when they are citizens.*

---

This is an issue that will definitely come to fore during the [Barack] Obama administration. With a Democrat-led Congress and the most liberal president in decades, I have no

Michael Vass, "Illegal Immigration: The Problem and a Potential Solution," MVass.com/MV Consulting, January 6, 2009. Reproduced by permission.

doubt that legislation will be attempted to give these criminals citizenship. I am completely against this idea.

Right now tens of millions if not more is being spent on illegal immigrants. Prosecuting illegal criminals, removing them from the work force, closing down sweatshops, medical aid, education and housing are but a few sources of the costs. While these individually are not major factors, combined they do help to affect the American economy. They add a burden that need not be there.

I have no problem with my taxes going to help those in need, when they are citizens. I have no problem helping people throughout the world. I endorse several humanitarian causes in Africa (Darfur among the top) and elsewhere. But those endorsements and donations are my choice. Illegal aliens are a burden I cannot choose to bear.

Think of it like this. I know of no one that would suggest that a crack-dealing-armed-robber should receive federal housing, unless that housing were a jail. But if that same individual was illegal some believe that criminal deserves—and some may have—federal housing. That is not to say that all illegal aliens are hardened criminals, but the fact is some are. And one dollar for that is a dollar too much.

---

*[Illegal immigrants] want to have rights of citizens, but are unwilling to accept the first responsibility of every citizen, following the law of the nation.*

---

There are those that believe illegal immigrant children deserve higher education. This is not elementary school or high school. They state that college is a right of these people, specifically the right to receive federal aid and in-state tuition, the same as American citizens. Which first ignores the willful act of being an active criminal in this nation. Second it grants rights we do not give to those that legally enter this nation for a higher education. And third it adds a burden that is not compensated for as these young adults (18–22) and their parents do not pay taxes which the financial aid comes from.

In the same vein of thought is everything that illegal immigrants demand and ask for. They want to have rights of citizens, but are unwilling to accept the first responsibility of every citizen, following the law of the nation. That is a bit backwards in logic.

Even more people wish to give these criminals a right to become citizens. To my knowledge America does not give criminals—especially those that have or would likely commit felonies—citizenship from any country. Every adult illegal alien has actively chosen to commit a felony and they want to be rewarded?

I do understand the difficulty in removing every illegal immigrant from the nation. Given the size and wealth of our nation (even in times of recession and depression, like now) it is unrealistic to believe we will ever remove or prevent all illegals. But that is not an excuse to place a value and commoditize our citizenship, which any plan or path to citizenship that involves a fine creates.

## Second-Class Citizenship

So what is the answer? Many will not like my answer. In fact to a degree I do not. Because it creates a de facto system of abuse. But the current system is basically no better in terms of abuse and/or discrimination.

But an idea is one that has worked in the ancient past. Secondary class citizens. We create a legal class of citizenship that is not entitled to every right just as a full citizen would receive.

All illegals that accept this would be entitled to continue to live and work in the nation.

- They do not have a right to vote.

- They do not have a right to federally funded housing.

- They do have a right to receive federally funded food and medical aid.

- Their illegal children have the same right to receive an education as any other citizen, but they cannot receive in-state college status.

- They can only receive half the federally funded financial aid of a citizen.

- They are protected by all the laws of a citizen, and must receive the pay of a citizen.

- They will pay 50% more in federal taxes which they must file for every year or have their status rescinded.

- Every illegal alien age 18–26 must sign up for a draft if the nation ever deems the need to call on them.

- And if they are convicted of any felony, ever, they will be deported immediately no matter if they have children that are citizens.

Those that would flaunt this choice, and try to avoid this, would be deported after losing all possessions and 1 year of hard labor (think chain gangs fixing roads across the nation).

Why might an illegal immigrant family or individual accept this? Because their children born on U.S. soil retain the rights of a full citizen. Because they will not be deported (so long as they do not violate the felony statute). Because even under these conditions they will live a quality of life greater than that in their home nations.

This plan is not completely fleshed out, so don't just tell me there are loopholes. I know there are, but I am not a politician and this is not a law I am presenting to Congress. This is an idea for others to iron out more completely. But it is comprehensive. And it addresses all illegal aliens currently in the nation and those to come. It is a path to citizenship, albeit to the children of the illegals. It removes the commoditization of U.S. citizenship and addresses the willful violation of our laws.

It's not nice, but life is not about nice. It's relatively fair, and far better than the lives they led in their homelands. And they always have the choice before them. They can leave or suffer the consequences of further violating our laws.

Now let the debate begin.

# The U.S. Government Should Prosecute Employers Who Hire Illegal Immigrants

*Eric Von Haessler*

*Eric Von Haessler is a radio show host in Atlanta, Georgia.*

The point that's gone unnoticed in the immigration debate currently twisting the 24-hour TV pundits into knots is that the whole problem could be solved within months. There is no immediate need for a fence, amnesty or a combination of the two. There is a solution that would work so fast the whole issue would disappear from national life as if into thin air.

## Dancing Around Immigration Solutions

The fact that the obvious solution is rarely, if ever, uttered— let alone acted on—can only lead the inquisitive to believe that actually solving the immigration problem isn't on the agenda of anyone with the power or authority to do so. This is politics as kabuki dance and nothing more. Each side is making the gestures it knows must be made, but it's all for the sake of the dance alone. Resolution of the problem doesn't even figure into it.

> *The prospect of a prolonged jail sentence will immediately get the attention of everyone present in every boardroom and construction trailer in America.*

Have you ever stopped to ask yourself why your government needs to waste time passing new laws concerning activ-

Eric Von Haessler, "Immigration? No Problem. The Point That's Gone Unnoticed in the Immigration Debate," *Sunday Paper*, July 1, 2007. Copyright © 2008 SundayPaper.com. Reproduced by permission.

ity that has already been deemed illegal? Living as an unde-
clared citizen in this country is illegal, and penalties for such
behavior have long been enshrined in state and federal law. So
why the need for new legislation? Why the need for a fence
now, when one wasn't needed for so long? The dance, my
friends. The dance.

Backers of a security fence envisioned to run some 700-
plus miles along the boundary between Mexico and America
claim the nonstop wave of humanity crossing the border is so
overwhelming that only a tall, solid structure can stop the invasion.

Supporters of amnesty argue that the forced and immediate deportation of 12 million souls would tear apart loving
families, and that the amount of displacement necessary to
pull it off would de facto become a cruel and unusual enterprise on the part of the government. In other words, they, like
their opponents who favor a wall, are saying that it's the overwhelming number of illegal aliens already here or coming
here that justifies their opposite, but equally radical, solution
to the problem.

## The Obvious Solution

If the politicians would stop dancing between constituencies
and start searching for clarity, they might just stumble upon
the easy way out. Instead of trying to stop the flow of humanity crossing into this country one by one, individual by individual, why not remove the thing they are coming for?

Remove the jobs and you remove the problem of immigration altogether. When applying the law in a situation like
this, it is important to apply it with the most force where it
will yield the most immediate results. An illegal immigrant,
on some level, has already come to terms with the fact that he
or she may end up dealing with law enforcement as a result of
his or her choices. The prospect of arrest and detention is
weighed against the potential revenue stream created if they

make it through. Immigrants make a risk/reward assessment that the possible consequences are worth the potential rewards.

The businessperson hiring that illegal immigrant, however, sees the world from a very different perspective. The prospect of a prolonged jail sentence will immediately get the attention of everyone present in every boardroom and construction trailer in America. Of course, fair notice must be given. After all, these people have been doing this with a wink and a nod from the government for years. We can be fair and still solve the problem.

In order to solve the "crisis" of illegal immigration, the federal government need only announce to business owners and CEOs that they have 90 days to stop using any and all undocumented workers. It further needs to be made clear that after this three-month reprieve, the Feds will begin arresting and prosecuting the most senior members of any business found in violation of immigration law.

It must be recognized that actually "solving" this problem may do more damage than good for the country: A $7 head of lettuce is the most probable outcome of all this. It's bound to get expensive once immigrant labor gets replaced by unionized workers demanding field masseuses for pickers who suffer lower back problems. But if you want it solved, it's solvable.

Send two or three millionaires to jail and the problem will go away overnight. Or just enjoy the dance. It's up to you.

# President Barack Obama Should Focus Immigration Enforcement on Employers and Criminals

*America's Voice*

*America's Voice is a communications campaign working to win commonsense immigration reform.*

It is now clear that the [George W.] Bush administration's priorities for immigration enforcement led to missed opportunities to strengthen immigration enforcement, crackdown on unscrupulous employers, and secure the border. The administration was distracted by a focus on garden variety immigration law violators rather than unscrupulous employers and dangerous criminals.

> *[President Bush's] immigration enforcement strategy focused intensely on punishing immigrant workers, while employers . . . were much less of a priority.*

The [Barack] Obama administration has a chance to redirect priorities toward the truly bad actors. Recently, Secretary of Homeland Security Janet Napolitano announced a new initiative focusing federal resources on combating the violent drug cartels in Mexico and weapons smuggling from the United States. And Napolitano has also indicated that her department will review the prior administration's controversial work site raids program and ensure that future efforts focus on unscrupulous employers who break labor and immigration laws.

Following is a review of the previous administration's immigration enforcement priorities, and analysis of the opportunities facing the current administration.

## Enforcement in the Workplace Targeted Workers, Not Employers

In the workplace, the Bush administration's immigration enforcement strategy focused intensely on punishing immigrant workers, while employers who broke labor and immigration laws were much less of a priority.

*In 2007, DHS' [Department of Homeland Security'] Immigration and Customs Enforcement (ICE) logged 4,077 administrative arrests and 863 criminal arrests at worksites across the country.*

In fiscal year [FY] 1999, 417 employers received notices of the government's intention to fine them for employing undocumented workers—a number that dropped to just three by 2004. After intense public scrutiny over this sharp decline in enforcement, Secretary of Homeland Security Michael Chertoff promised that "The days of treating employers who violate [immigration] laws by giving them the equivalent of a corporate parking ticket—those days are gone. It's now felonies, jail time, fines, and forfeitures." Yet the number of employers receiving notices of the Department's intent to fine grew to just seventeen in 2007.

In 2007, DHS's [Department of Homeland Security's] Immigration and Customs Enforcement (ICE) logged 4,077 administrative arrests and 863 criminal arrests at work sites across the country. Only 92 of the criminal arrests were of employers or managers. Immigrant workers accounted for 98% of all workplace immigration arrests and 89% of all workplace criminal arrests in FY 2007. The story was much the same in FY 2008, when ICE made nearly 5,200 administrative arrests and 1,101 criminal arrests. Only 135 of ICE's criminal arrests in FY 2008 were of employers or managers. This means that immigrant workers made up 98% of all work site immigration arrests and 87% of work site criminal arrests in FY 2008 as well.

Studies by the Government Accountability Office (GAO) also show that labor law enforcement suffered under the Bush administration. A July 2008 study found that the Department of Labor (DOL) "inadequately investigated complaints from low wage and minimum wage workers alleging that employers failed to pay the federal minimum wage, required overtime, and failed to pay employees their last paychecks." Another report in 2009 found that DOL's Wage and Hour Division [WHD] mishandled nine out of ten wage theft cases the GAO used to evaluate the division's performance.

The notorious Agriprocessors case is one example of how the Bush administration focused its enforcement efforts on the wrong target. In May 2008, ICE raided the Agriprocessors meat packing plant in Postville, Iowa, and arrested nearly 400 immigrant workers. Over 300 of the workers were charged with crimes related to working without papers, and shuttled through cookie-cutter plea deals to serve time in prison before deportation. For years before the raid, company owners and managers had been accused of serious labor abuses including wage and hour violations, employing underage labor, coercion, and more. In fact, they were being investigated for some of these violations by the state labor department at the time ICE raided the plant.

But rather than throw the book at the employer, who had clearly used the broken immigration system to commit very serious labor violations, ICE focused its efforts on prosecuting, detaining, and deporting the plant's workers. Only after six months of intense public pressure did the Bush administration finally bring charges against the former CEO of Agriprocessors for his role in procuring the fake documents used by workers at the plant. But the rest of the labor abuses have gone unpunished by the federal government, and victims of serious labor and criminal law violations would be unable to testify because they were deported.

## Enforcement in the Field Targeted Workers, Not Criminals

Reports by the Immigration Justice Clinic at the Benjamin N. Cardozo School of Law and the Migration Policy Institute show that ICE's Fugitive Operations Teams also made a dangerous shift in priorities over the last several years. Fugitive Operations Teams (FOTs) are made up of seven to eight ICE agents each, and are charged with finding and arresting foreign nationals who were scheduled to be deported but have remained in the United States. They often work with state and local police in doing so. Before 2006, the Bush administration tasked each FOT with arresting 125 "high priority" targets each year, requiring that at least 75% of the arrests focus on criminals who have violated deportation orders. However, under pressure to appear "tough" on immigration enforcement, in 2006 the Bush administration issued a directive that established a new quota of 1,000 arrests per FOT, and removed the 75% threshold for criminal targets.

---

*The federal government dramatically stepped up criminal prosecutions of immigrant workers, instead of focusing in on violent offenders and white-collar criminals.*

---

According to the Migration Policy Institute, despite a mandate from Congress "to arrest dangerous fugitives, almost three-quarters (73 percent) of the individuals apprehended by FOTs from 2003 through February 2008 had no criminal conviction." Similarly, the Immigration Justice Clinic at the Benjamin N. Cardozo School of Law found that since the 2006 shift in priorities, FOT arrests of undocumented immigrants with no criminal record went up 32%. The study's authors concluded that "while the human costs of ICE's home raid strategy were painfully high, the law enforcement gains were shockingly low."

Not only did ICE target undocumented workers over criminals through its Fugitive Operations Teams, but the federal government dramatically stepped up criminal prosecutions of immigrant workers, instead of focusing in on violent offenders and white-collar criminals. The Transactional Records Access Clearinghouse (TRAC) at Syracuse University reported recently that "federal prosecutions of immigration crimes nearly doubled in the last fiscal year, reaching more than 70,000 immigration cases in the 2008 fiscal year." Meanwhile, federal prosecutions for white-collar crime fell by 15% from 2000 to 2008, and drug prosecutions were down 20% from FY 2001 to FY 2008.

---

*The Bush administration also reduced programs to assist state and local police in fighting crime, and directed money toward expanding their role in civil immigration enforcement.*

---

"Operation Streamline," a program requiring the prosecution of undocumented workers for the crime of entering without inspection, is responsible for much of this shift. Instituted in 2005, the program has been quite controversial among judges, prosecutors, and others because it prioritizes immigration enforcement over more serious crimes. George P. Kazen, the senior judge in Laredo (Texas), told the *New York Times* he was concerned about other priorities getting short shrift, including weapons smuggling from the United States to Mexico by drug cartels. "The U.S. attorney isn't bringing me those cases. They're just catching foot soldiers coming across the border. They bust some stooge truck driver carrying a load of drugs, and you know there's more behind it. But they will tell you that they don't have the resources to drive it and develop a conspiracy case."

In fact, former U.S. attorney for the Southern California district Carol C. Lam was ousted after refusing to supplant more serious cases for low-grade immigration offenses. Lam told the *New York Times*: "If two-thirds of a U.S. attorney's office is handling low-level narcotics and immigration crimes, young prosecutors may not have the opportunity to learn how to do a wiretap case, or learn how to deal with the grand jury, or how to use money laundering statutes or flip witnesses or deal with informants and undercover investigations. That's not good law enforcement."

## Federal Support to State and Local Police Declines

The Bush administration also reduced programs to assist state and local police in fighting crime, and directed money toward expanding their role in civil immigration enforcement.

Funding for the State Criminal Alien Assistance Program (SCAAP)—a reimbursement program for state and local law enforcement agencies that detain foreign nationals convicted of crimes—declined precipitously during the Bush years from $573 million in FY 2000 to a low of $240 million in FY 2003 (the FY 2008 appropriation was increased to $410 million). According to a report by the University of Arizona for the U.S./Mexico Border Counties Coalition, the twenty-four U.S. counties along our nation's border with Mexico incurred $192 million in law enforcement and criminal justice costs related to undocumented immigration in FY 2006, adding up to a total of $1.23 billion from 1999 through 2006. However, the federal government only reimbursed these counties $4.7 million through SCAAP in FY 2006, for a total of $54.8 million from 1999 to 2006.

In fact, the Bush administration tried to terminate SCAAP, zeroing it out of the president's annual budget year after year. The program was saved through concerted advocacy by state and local police, governors, other elected officials, and members of Congress, but suffered serious hits that put more of the financial burden on states and localities. President Obama's FY 2009 budget request also leaves out SCAAP, according to the U.S./Mexico Border Counties Coalition.

Other federal initiatives created to support state and local police, such as the Community Oriented Policing Services (COPS) program, were also underfunded over the last several years. For example, in FY 2008 COPS funding stood at less than half of its original appropriation ($587 million versus $1.3 billion in FY 1995). According to analysis by Third Way, federal criminal justice aid to states fell a whopping 56% during the current decade.

---

*Many in law enforcement believe that involving state and local police in the deportation of noncriminal, undocumented workers makes it harder for them . . . to solve real crimes.*

---

Meanwhile, Congress allocated $42 million for the 287(g) program in FY 2008, an increase of $27 million over the previous year. 287(g) is a program where state and local law enforcement agencies can enter into agreements with the federal government, receive training, and be deputized to enforce civil immigration laws. Most of the money appropriated for the program funds the training of police officers in immigration law, not the costs of implementing the agreements at the state and local level. In addition, many in law enforcement believe that involving state and local police in the deportation of noncriminal, undocumented workers makes it harder for them to work with the community to solve real crimes and put criminals behind bars.

Recently, Montgomery County (Maryland) Police Chief J. Thomas Manger testified on behalf of the Major Cities Chiefs Association in a hearing on the 287(g) program before the House Committee on Homeland Security. Manger said that: "Immigration enforcement by local police would likely negatively affect and undermine the level of trust and cooperation between local police and immigrant communities.... Without assurances that contact with the police would not result in purely civil immigration-enforcement action, the hard-won trust, communication and cooperation from the immigrant community would disappear. Such a divide between the local police and immigrant groups would result in increased crime against immigrants and in the broader community, create a class of silent victims, and eliminate the potential for assistance from immigrants in solving crimes or preventing future terroristic acts."

The Obama administration should recommit to programs like SCAAP and COPS that have suffered over the last several years. The American Recovery and Reinvestment Act of 2009 wisely included $1 billion for the COPS Hiring Recovery Program, so that the current economic crisis does not lead to fewer cops on the street. However, more must be done to ensure state and local police resources are directed at real criminals and dangerous individuals, not civil enforcement duties that take police away from their primary mission of fighting crime.

## A More Sensible Approach

In each of the areas examined—immigration law enforcement, labor law enforcement, and support to state and local police— the Bush administration focused its resources on immigrant workers rather than unscrupulous employers and dangerous criminals, and missed an opportunity [to] target the truly bad actors.

The Obama administration should pursue effective immigration enforcement strategies that are focused like a laser on the worst offenders—the employers who use our broken immigration system to undercut workers and law-abiding competitors, the criminals who hide in the shadows, and the smugglers who profit from our broken immigration system. In addition, Congress and the administration should pass a comprehensive immigration reform law that brings undocumented workers out of the shadows and requires them to go through background checks, pay fines and back taxes, and learn English on the way to earning U.S. citizenship.

According to the Coalition for Immigration Security, a group of former federal law enforcement officials concerned about effective enforcement: "The current flow of illegal immigrants and people overstaying their visas has made it extremely difficult for our border and interior enforcement agencies to be able to focus on the terrorists, organized criminals, and violent felons who use the cloak of anonymity that the current chaotic situation offers. . . . But enforcement alone will not do the job of securing our borders. Enforcement at the border will only be successful in the long-term if it is coupled with a more sensible approach to the 10–12 million illegal aliens in the country today and the many more who will attempt to migrate into the United States for economic reasons."

# The United States Should Enforce Labor Rights for Illegal Immigrants

*Bill Ong Hing and David Bacon*

*Bill Ong Hing is a professor at the University of California Davis School of Law. David Bacon is an associate editor at Pacific News Service and the author of several books on immigration.*

When the [Barack] Obama administration reiterated recently that it will make an immigration reform proposal this year [2009], hopes rose among millions of immigrant families for the "change we can believe in." That was followed by a new immigration position embraced by both the AFL-CIO [American Federation of Labor and Congress of Industrial Organizations] and the Change to Win unions, rejecting the expansion of guest worker programs, which some unions had supported.

As it prepares a reform package, the administration should look seriously at why the deals created over the past several years failed, and consider alternatives. Beltway [referring to the freeway that encircles Washington, D.C.] groups are again proposing employment visas for future labor shortages and continued imprisonment of the undocumented [workers] in detention centers, which they deem "necessary in some cases." Most disturbing, after years of the [President George W.] Bush raids, is the continued emphasis on enforcement against workers.

We need a reality check.

## The Failure of Immigration Raids and Employer Sanctions

For more than two decades it has been a crime for an undocumented worker to hold a job in the United States. To enforce the prohibition, agents conduct immigration raids, of the kind we saw at meat packing plants in the past few years.

---

*[Immigration enforcement] measures all enforce a provision ... employer sanctions—which makes it illegal for an employer to hire a worker with no legal immigration status.*

---

Today, some suggest "softer," or more politically palatable, enforcement—a giant database of Social Security numbers (E-Verify). Employers would be able to hire only those whose numbers "verify" their legal immigration status. Workers without such "work authorization" would have to be fired.

Whether hard or soft, these measures all enforce a provision of immigration law on the books since 1986—employer sanctions—which makes it illegal for an employer to hire a worker with no legal immigration status. In reality, the law makes it a crime for an undocumented worker to have a job.

The rationale has always been that this will dry up jobs for the undocumented and discourage them from coming. Those of us who served on a United Food and Commercial Workers commission that studied Immigration and Customs Enforcement (ICE) raids at Swift meat packing plants across the country learned that the law has had disastrous effects on all workers. Instead of reinforcing or tweaking employer sanctions, we would be much better off if we ended them.

Raids and workplace enforcement have left severe emotional scars on families. Workers were mocked. Children were separated from their parents and left without word at schools or day care. Increased enforcement has poisoned communities, spawning scores of state and local anti-immigrant laws and ordinances that target workers and their families.

---

*Attempting to discourage workers from coming by arresting them for working without authorization, or trying to prevent them from finding work, is doomed to fail.*

---

Employer sanctions have failed to reduce undocumented migration because NAFTA [North American Free Trade Agreement] and globalization create huge migration pressure. Since 1994 more than 6 million Mexicans have come to the United States. Ismael Rojas, who arrived without papers, says, "You can either abandon your children to make money to take care of them, or you can stay with your children and watch them live in misery. Poverty makes us leave our families."

Attempting to discourage workers from coming by arresting them for working without authorization, or trying to prevent them from finding work, is doomed to fail. To reduce the pressure that causes undocumented migration, we need to change our trade and economic policies so they don't produce poverty in countries like Mexico.

Ken Georgetti, president of the Canadian Labour Congress, and AFL-CIO president John Sweeney wrote to President [Barack] Obama and Canadian prime minister [Stephen] Harper, reminding them that "the failure of neoliberal policies to create decent jobs in the Mexican economy under NAFTA has meant that many displaced workers and new entrants have been forced into a desperate search to find employment elsewhere." The new joint position of the AFL-CIO and Change to Win federations recognizes that "an essential component of the long-term solution is a fair trade and globalization model that uplifts all workers."

Continued support for work authorization and employer sanctions contradicts this understanding. Even with a legalization program, millions of people will remain without papers.

For them, work without "authorization" will still be a crime. And while employer sanctions have little effect on migration, they will continue to make workers vulnerable to employer pressure.

When undocumented workers are fired for protesting low wages and bad conditions, employer sanctions bar them from receiving unemployment or disability benefits, although the workers have paid for them. It's much harder for them to find another job. An E-Verify database to deny them work will make this problem much worse.

Workplace enforcement also increases discrimination. Four years after sanctions began, the Government Accountability Office reported that 346,000 US employers applied immigration-verification requirements only to job applicants with a "foreign" accent or appearance. Another 430,000 only hired US-born applicants.

---

*The alternative to employer sanctions is enforcing the right to organize, minimum wage, overtime and other worker protection laws.*

---

## The Need for Labor Rights Enforcement

Despite these obstacles, immigrant workers, including the un-documented, have asserted their labor rights, organized unions and won better conditions. But employer sanctions have made this harder and riskier. When raids and document verification terrorized immigrants at Smithfield's huge packinghouse in Tar Heel, North Carolina, it became harder for black and white workers to organize as well. Using Social Security numbers to verify immigration status makes the firing and black-listing of union activists all but inevitable. Citizens and permanent residents feel this impact because in our diverse workplaces, immigrant and native-born workers work together.

Low wages for undocumented workers will rise only if those workers can organize. The Employee Free Choice Act would make organizing easier for all workers. But "work authorization" will rob millions of immigrant workers of their ability to use the process that act would establish.

The alternative to employer sanctions is enforcing the right to organize, minimum wage, overtime and other worker protection laws. Eliminating sanctions will not change the requirement that people immigrate here legally. ICE will still have the power to enforce immigration law. And if a fair legalization program were passed at the same time sanctions were eliminated, many undocumented workers already here would normalize their status. A more generous policy for issuing residence and family unification visas would allow families to cross the border legally, without the indentured servitude of guest worker programs.

Immigrant rights plus jobs programs that require employers to hire from communities with high unemployment can reduce competition and fear. Together they would strengthen unions, raise incomes, contribute to the nation's economic recovery and bring the people of our country together. Employer sanctions will continue to tear us apart.

# CHAPTER 4

# How Should U.S. Immigration Policy Be Reformed?

# Chapter Preface

In 2006 and 2007, policy makers in the United States tried but failed to pass immigration reform legislation. Republican and Democrat Senate leaders joined with President George W. Bush in support of what was called "comprehensive immigration reform." The goal was to overhaul immigration law with a package of reforms viewed as a compromise between pro-immigration advocates who sought to protect illegal immigrants and anti-immigration forces who wanted to see better enforcement of U.S. immigration laws. The main bill, called the Secure Borders, Economic Opportunity and Immigration Reform Act of 2007 (S. 1348), would have awarded legal status and a path to citizenship for the approximately 12 million illegal immigrants currently residing in the country—a program many referred to as amnesty. At the same time, the bill provided for increased border enforcement—more border fencing, high-tech surveillance equipment, and 20,000 more border patrol agents. If passed, the law also would have created a temporary guest worker program and would have made a number of other changes in immigration laws.

First introduced in the U.S. Senate on May 9, 2007, S. 1348 was reintroduced a second time as S. 1639 after facing resistance, but the legislation soon died without ever coming to a vote a short time later. Observers said the controversy surrounding the reforms was simply too polarized, and instead of uniting the differing sides of the immigration debate, the legislation seemed only to highlight the divisions. Conservatives criticized the amnesty aspect of the bill, for example, while liberals found fault with the guest worker program and other reform provisions. In the end, a bipartisan majority prevented legislation from moving to a final vote. Later, Congress passed a more limited bill authorizing many of the increased border enforcement elements of S. 1348.

In 2009, the newly elected U.S. president Barack Obama pledged to once again seek comprehensive immigration reforms. Some commentators have suggested that Obama is committed to act on immigration because of the strong support he received during the 2008 presidential campaign from Latinos, who turned out in record numbers to vote for him and other Democrats. Whatever the motivation, the new legislative effort began in April 2009 when Senator Charles Schumer (D-NY), head of a Senate immigration subcommittee, held hearings on the issue. According to reports, U.S. Congress will introduce a new immigration bill early in Obama's presidency.

Many commentators, however, believe that the next round of debate about immigration may be just as contentious as the last time. Some people think the issue may even be more difficult because of the economic recession that has gripped the United States. Many observers predict that rising unemployment among Americans will cause the public to be very concerned about illegal immigrants taking American jobs. Economic difficulties could also create more of a xenophobic backlash, adding to the pressure on legislators to crack down on illegal immigration. Others say, however, that the recession is causing fewer foreign workers to come to the United States seeking work, and that as a result, immigration is less of a concern to many Americans than it was in 2007.

Apart from the new economic factors, the immigration debate is expected to focus on many of the same issues confronted earlier. One of these issues is what to do about the 12 million illegal immigrants already living in the United States. Most observers expect that any proposal drafted by the Democrats will most likely again contain some type of amnesty program and offer legal status and eventual citizenship to resident illegal immigrants, but such a plan will likely once again face bitter opposition. Critics think amnesty is inherently unfair, since it rewards illegal conduct, and that it will only encourage more immigrants to enter the United States illegally in the hopes of gaining U.S. citizenship. One important difference this time, however, is that amnesty will have the support of a very popular and effective president. Obama has already signaled that he supports some type of amnesty to move illegal workers out of the shadows and decrease the risk that they can be exploited by U.S. employers.

Another important issue will be how to improve immigration enforcement, whether that means enhanced border security or better internal enforcement. So far, the new administration has embraced a nuanced approach to enforcement. On the one hand, the government is moving forward with a controversial virtual border fence project, and administration officials announced in May 2009 that they want local jails to check the immigration status of all prisoners. Federal and state prisons already perform such checks, but having local jails do so is expected to greatly increase the numbers of illegal immigrant criminals found and deported. At the same time, however, the administration has appointed a number of illegal immigrant advocates to key positions, and Janet Napolitano, secretary of homeland security, has indicated that the government is suspending the workplace immigration raids favored by the Bush administration. Instead, the administration has announced that it will focus its enforcement efforts on businesses and executives who hire illegal immigrants. How this will be accomplished is not yet completely clear, but part of the plan may be to require employers to use an electronic system of verification to check on the immigration status of potential employees before they are hired. A voluntary verification system, called E-Verify, has already been set up and is being used by an increasing number of employers. Although many immigrants' rights advocates oppose the program, Napolitano expressed the administration's support for E-Verify in a May 2009 congressional hearing.

A third stumbling block for immigration reform concerns whether to create or expand guest worker programs for both unskilled and highly skilled immigrants. U.S. business interests have long sought to create a new guest worker program, arguing that foreign workers are needed to perform low-skill jobs that American workers do not want, such as picking fruits and vegetables and working in meat processing plants. Meanwhile, high-tech companies, such as Microsoft, advocate expansion of the H-1B visa program for skilled workers. State and local governments and many concerned citizens, however, believe that allowing more immigrants into the country, whether through illegal immigration or through temporary visa programs, places a burden on hospitals and public schools, which are mandated to provide services to all residents regardless of immigration status. These public costs, critics say, should not be born by the taxpayers to benefit large corporate employers. Obama has signaled that he does not favor expanding guest worker programs.

As immigration reform moves forward, the president and Congress are likely to hear a number of competing proposals for how it should be done. The viewpoints in this chapter set forth some of the many immigration reform ideas and suggestions circulating as this critical public debate continues.

# Congress Should Stem Both Illegal and Legal Immigration

*Federation for American Immigration Reform*

*The Federation for American Immigration Reform (FAIR) is a national, nonprofit membership organization dedicated to reforming the nation's immigration policies.*

The evidence that illegal immigration and mass immigration are harming our country is overwhelming and irrefutable. The American family is increasingly bearing the costs of traffic congestion, urban sprawl, environmental degradation, increased crime, overburdened health care, overwhelmed public schools, and debt-ridden state and municipal governments. The fiscal cost of immigration—both legal and illegal—has always been substantial, but with the recent economic downturn, these costs have become even more burdensome to the American taxpayer. The 111th Congress [January 3, 2009 until January 3, 2011] has both the opportunity and the obligation to address these problems by enforcing existing laws that would stem the tide of illegal immigration and also passing new legislation that will curtail legal immigration and improve national security and quality of life.

## Deadlock in the 110th Congress

The first summer of the 110th Congress saw two attempts by the [George W.] Bush administration and a handful of senators to pass a comprehensive immigration reform bill—legislation that included amnesty for illegal aliens, expansion of guest worker programs, and an increase of green cards. The debates lasted for days with senators from both sides of the aisle proposing amendments to strip the legislation of its con-

*An Immigration Reform Agenda for the 111th Congress.* Washington, DC: Federation for American Immigration Reform, 2009. Reproduced by permission.

troversial amnesty and visa expansion programs. Throughout the debate, citizens across the country were vocal in their opposition, fighting tooth and nail to defeat the bill and going so far as to shut down the Senate switchboard with a large volume of calls. In the end, the bill twice failed to pass a cloture vote, leaving the coalition that drafted the bill fractured and grassroots activists across the country engaged and invigorated after their efforts to defeat the bill were ultimately realized.

Following defeat of the 2007 amnesty bill, a stalemate arose in the 110th Congress between those who wanted to increase immigration and impose a mass amnesty program upon our nation and those who wanted to fix our broken borders and implement reforms to protect American workers, national security and the environment. Perhaps the single greatest illustration of the deadlock was Congress's inability to reauthorize the popular E-Verify program [which provides employers a process for checking the immigration status of workers] for more than six months. The voluntary program is overwhelmingly supported by the American people, but after passing the House with only two dissenting votes, E-Verify reauthorization stalled when one senator attempted to condition its passage with an addition of more than 550,000 extra employment and family based visas.

Despite deadlocks in the 110th Congress over unpopular visa expansion programs and popular programs such as E-Verify, immigration reformers scored some legislative victories. For example, the FY [fiscal year] 2009 Homeland Security Appropriations bill included $14.81 billion for Customs and Border Protection (CBP) and Immigration and Customs Enforcement (ICE), which exceeded the president's request for the two departments by $588 million. The funding increase allows for an additional 2,200 border patrol agents and $775 million for border security, fencing, infrastructure and technology. While these funding measures are meaningful and necessary, they are by themselves inadequate without an underlying legislative plan.

The close of the 110th Congress coincided with an economic downturn that left much of the nation shocked, national leadership scrambling for a rescue plan, and multiple states and municipalities announcing large budget deficits and hiring freezes. The 111th Congress must pick up where the 110th Congress left off, continuing enforcement of the nation's existing immigration laws and making passage of true immigration reform legislation a top priority.

---

*As [the illegal alien population] ... has expanded rapidly in the last few decades, the immigration reform debate has understandably become centered on stopping illegal immigration.*

---

Within FAIR's [Federation for American Immigration Reform] legislative agenda for the 111th Congress, there are three major areas of immigration reform: illegal immigration reform, national security reform, and legal immigration reform. These reforms often overlap and many of the suggested policy solutions for one area will prove to address all three areas of immigration policy. The lists of suggested reforms are by no means exhaustive, but do represent reforms FAIR considers to be top priorities and the most effective solutions for solving the immigration crisis in the United States.

## Illegal Immigration Reform

The illegal alien population in the United States—estimated by FAIR to be around 13 million—is comprised of people illegally crossing the border and overstaying their visas. As this number has expanded rapidly in the last few decades, the immigration reform debate has understandably become centered on stopping illegal immigration. Securing the borders, implementing a proper entry and exit system for visa holders, and denying jobs to illegal aliens are key components for ending illegal immigration—each of which must be properly addressed. In addition to opposing all efforts to grant amnesty to illegal aliens, the 111th Congress should seek to end illegal immigration by implementing the following illegal immigration reforms.

*Work Site Enforcement.* There is overwhelming consensus that most illegal aliens come to the United States for economic reasons, which makes work site enforcement programs a vital step toward true immigration reform. Recently, ICE officials have stepped up their efforts to enforce employment laws across the country, and FAIR applauds their efforts as the presence of illegal aliens in the workforce serves to depress normal wages and take jobs from U.S. citizens. These work site enforcement operations must be continued and expanded in order to guarantee a legal workforce and protect American workers. To ensure a legal workforce, Congress should implement the following measures:

- Permanently authorize the E-Verify program and provide adequate funding to guarantee the future of the program

- Make the E-Verify program mandatory for all existing and new hires

- Support ICE work site enforcement operations with more agents and increased funding to allow for more detention beds

- Permit U.S. citizens and legal permanent residents to file unfair employment practices under the Immigration and Nationality Act (INA)

- Permit civil actions by employers against other employers who intentionally fail to verify work eligibility of their employees

- Increase and consistently apply civil and criminal penalties against employers of illegal aliens

---

*Document fraud is one of the primary ways illegal aliens manipulate the system to stay in the United States and gain employment.*

---

*Ensure a Secure Identification System.* Document fraud is one of the primary ways illegal aliens manipulate the system to stay in the United States and gain employment. Fraudulent birth certificates, driver's licenses, and immigration documents enable illegal aliens to obtain employment and, in some instances, claim benefits for which they would otherwise be ineligible. Moreover, hundreds of thousands of fraudulent or stolen Social Security numbers (SSN) are submitted to the Social Security Administration (SSA) each year, which severely impacts the lives of the U.S. citizens and legal aliens whose numbers are stolen. To create secure and tamper proof identification documents, FAIR advocates the following measures:

- Secure the Social Security card by making it counterfeit proof and tamper-resistant

- Increase and implement use of biometrics for all immigration documents

- Appropriate sufficient funds and enforce state deadlines for the implementation of REAL ID

- Encourage states to require proof of legal presence for the issuance of driver's licenses by denying federal transportation dollars to states that fail to do so

- Authorize and fund increased training for federal, state, and local law enforcement officers on the detection of fraudulent documents

- Bar the use of Matricula Consular cards [identification cards issued by the Mexican government] for purposes of establishing identity, especially for illegal aliens opening bank accounts and applying for access to government benefits

*Support State and Local Efforts.* State and local law enforcement and government agencies play a crucial role in ending illegal immigration, and it is important they be assured they have the proper support from the federal government to arrest, detain, and transfer illegal aliens. To improve the enforcement of immigration laws at the state and local level, FAIR advocates the following measures:

- Support the 287(g) program by ensuring adequate funding and training for all interested local law enforcement agencies

- Fully reimburse state and local law enforcement expenses directly related to illegal immigration (except where local sanctuary policies encourage illegal immigration)

*Federal Agency Reform.* The federal agencies responsible for overseeing immigration programs and enforcement efforts do not have sufficient permission or resources to share information and cooperate with each other, which substantially hinders their ability to perform their respective tasks. To improve their effectiveness, FAIR advocates the following reforms:

- Require the SSA to share information with the Department of Homeland Security (DHS) on issuance of no-match letters to employers and of suspicious employment use of legitimate SSNs

- Restrict the use of Individual Taxpayer Identification Numbers (ITINs) to tax-related purposes only

- Require the Internal Revenue Service (IRS) to investigate and apply sanctions for fraudulent tax documents submitted by employers and aliens

- Reform tax laws to penalize employers who use the employment of illegal aliens to their advantage (i.e., deduction of wages and benefits)

- Ensure that work performed by illegal aliens will not count toward Social Security regardless of future changes in that alien's immigration status

- Increase the number of immigration judges employed by the Department of Justice (DOJ) and set standards for training that specifically includes identity fraud

- Increase the number of asylum officers employed by DHS and set standards for training that specifically includes identity fraud

---

*The undetected presence of 19 foreign nationals ... who carried out the 9/11 [2001] attacks demonstrated that immigration law ... is an integral aspect of national security policy.*

---

*Oppose Efforts to Give Benefits to Illegal Aliens.* Benefits to illegal aliens amount to nothing more than taxpayer subsidies of criminal behavior and serve only to encourage more illegal immigration. With the exception of emergency medical care, illegal aliens are ineligible for most federally administered benefits. However, many states have not adopted similar provisions barring illegal aliens from state and local benefits. The 111th Congress should refuse to allow federal taxpayer dollars to subsidize state policies that encourage illegal immigration. To limit taxpayer-funded benefits to illegal aliens, FAIR advocates enacting the following measures:

- Support efforts to eliminate sanctuary cities by withholding federal funding from localities that enact such policies or practices

- Protect legal students and taxpayers by opposing congressional efforts to permit states to give illegal aliens in-state tuition at public universities and community colleges

- Withhold federal grants to public universities that enroll aliens who have neither legal residence nor a valid visa

- Require employers to reimburse states for education, health care, and other services used by legal temporary workers

- Oppose amnesty for illegal aliens

## National Security Reform

The undetected presence of the 19 foreign nationals in the United States who carried out the 9/11 [2001] attacks demonstrated that immigration law—the regulation of who enters our country under what conditions and for what length of time—is an integral aspect of national security policy. 9/11 affirmed what FAIR had been warning for years: if the country is to remain secure and sovereign, immigration and customs officers and U.S. law enforcement officials must be able to quickly and efficiently ascertain which aliens are in the country legally. The 111th Congress must work with enforcement agencies using infrastructure and technology to further secure U.S. borders and develop new methods for screening and admitting aliens to the country.

*Secure the Borders and Ports of Entry.* A fundamental step to solving our illegal immigration problem and ensuring our national security is to secure the borders and ports of entry. More than one million illegal aliens have been apprehended annually at the border in recent years, and the problems of gang violence and drug and weapon trafficking continue to plague the southern border. Until sufficient resources, infrastructure, and manpower are placed at the border, these problems will persist. FAIR advocates the following border security measures:

- Appropriate sufficient funds to realize border security efforts

- Complete the physical fence on the southern border

- Increase the number of border patrol agents, customs agents, etc., along the border

- Equip border states and local law enforcement to manage border-related issues

- Increase detention space to prevent resumption of catch-and-release policies

- Increase manpower at all ports of entry to provide for thorough screening of all entrants

- Oppose all efforts to implement the cross-border trucking program with Mexico

*Implement a Secure and Efficient Admission and Removal Process.* Despite recent advances in obtaining, checking and retaining biometric and other information on arriving foreign travelers, a major gap in a comprehensive entry-exit system persists. Currently, the processes and procedures for determining who is ineligible for admission and removing aliens who are present in the United States are inefficient and contain many loopholes, including wide judicial discretion. To help create a secure admissions and removal system, FAIR advocates the following measures:

- Fully implement US-VISIT [an immigration and border management system] to provide for a comprehensive entry-exit system

- Prohibit the granting of immigration benefits until all background checks of applicants are completed to the satisfaction of DHS

- Repeal the Visa Waiver Program

- Require all immigrant visa applicants to go through complete background checks

- Deny visas to nationals of countries that deny repatriation of their citizens

- Streamline processes for immigration litigation

- Restrict temporary protected status (TPS) to persons legally present in the United States when the event occurs that leads to the requested temporary protection

- Reform the TPS, asylum, and refugee programs to prohibit granting such status to gang members

- Authorize the detention of dangerous aliens

- Implement biometric screening for all aliens at all ports of entry

---

*A sustainable level of immigration is no more than 300,000 annually.*

---

## Legal Immigration Reform

The population of the United States has dramatically increased over the past few decades, and with that increase has come rises in petroleum, food, and other commodity prices and shortages of such natural resources as fresh air and water. This population growth is integrally connected to the nation's current immigration policies—policies which, if not dramatically reformed, will continue to result in unsustainable population growth. In fact, a recent report released by the U.S. Census Bureau warns that the United States will have 135 million more people in 2050 than it does today if current population and immigration trends continue. These drastic population increases affect the quality of life for every American and, in addition to environmental impacts, raise serious concerns about school systems, infrastructure needs, state budgets, and health care costs. Fortunately, it is not too late to curb population growth and prevent irreparable environmental degradation. To help stem population growth, the 111th Congress should prevent growth of guest worker programs, end the chain migration policies that give preferential treatment to adult family members, and categorically oppose efforts to give amnesty to illegal aliens.

*Cut the Numbers.* The United States currently admits over one million legal permanent residents every year—the equivalent of annually adding a city the size of Detroit. FAIR believes that a sustainable level of immigration is no more than 300,000 annually. To cut the numbers while allowing for the maintenance of nuclear families, FAIR advocates the following measures:

- Eliminate birthright citizenship legislatively

- Repeal the visa lottery

- Grant immigrant visas to skilled workers and deny visas to unskilled workers

- Restrict family preference visas to nuclear family members (spouse and minor children)

- Oppose any efforts to reauthorize INA §245(i)

*Stop Legal Immigration Fraud.* The United States has a rich history of immigration that is unfortunately undermined by high levels of fraud within the refugee, asylum, and visa systems. The United States must maintain the credibility of its immigration laws by exercising greater discretion in admitting immigrants and ensuring that the asylum program serves the population for which it was intended. To restore integrity to the immigration system, FAIR recommends the following measures:

- Impose stricter standards for the admission and removal of guest workers

- Reform or eliminate immigration programs with notably high rates of fraud (i.e., TPS and asylum, H-1B visas, religious worker visas, etc.)

*Protect the American Worker.* U.S. immigration laws already contain a multitude of guest worker programs, including programs for unskilled workers, agricultural workers, high-tech workers, and nurses. Given the current economic situation, the 111th Congress should take special care to protect the American worker by restricting the amount of cheap, foreign labor that is allowed to compete with U.S. workers. To ensure a legal workforce, FAIR advocates the following measures:

- Require that U.S. workers be given absolute preference in hiring and against layoffs

- Oppose all visa expansion programs

- Reform existing guest worker programs by cutting the numbers and opposing new programs

# The United States Should Create More Opportunities for Legal Immigration

## Jason L. Riley

*Jason L. Riley is a member of the editorial board of the* Wall Street Journal, *an American financial and business newspaper. He is also the author of the book,* Let Them In: The Case for Open Borders.

When President Barack Obama turns his attention to immigration reform later this year [2009], he will be pressured by advocacy groups and fellow Democrats to focus on a legalization program for the 12 million or so undocumented immigrants already living in the United States. Obviously, the plight of this illegal population must be part of any policy discussion. But if Mr. Obama wants to be more successful than the previous administration when it tried to reform immigration, he should avoid getting bogged down in a debate over "amnesty."

> *Illegal immigration to the United States is primarily a function of too many foreigners chasing too few visas.*

Critics of comprehensive immigration reform, which ideally combines legalization with more visas and more enforcement measures, say that the last amnesty enacted—the Immigration Reform and Control Act (IRCA) of 1986—didn't solve the illegal alien problem. This is true but misleading. After all, border enforcement enhancements over the past two decades haven't stanched the illegal flow, either, but that hasn't stopped immigration restrictionists from calling for still more security measures.

## Too Few Visas

The reality is that the 1986 amnesty was never going to solve the problem, because it didn't address the root cause. Illegal immigration to the United States is primarily a function of too many foreigners chasing too few visas. Some 400,000 people enter the country illegally each year—a direct consequence of the fact that our current policy is to make available only 5,000 visas annually for low-skilled workers. If policy makers want to reduce the number of illegal entries, the most sensible and humane course is to provide more legal ways for people to come.

---

*From a public policy perspective, the fate of the 12 million illegals already here is largely a side issue, a problem that will solve itself over time if we get the other reforms right.*

---

This could be done by creating viable guest worker programs or increasing green card quotas or both. The means matter less than the end, which should be to give U.S. businesses legal access to foreign workers going forward. The 1986 amnesty legislation didn't do that, which is why it didn't solve the problem.

The three million illegal aliens who were brought into legal status under IRCA had already been absorbed by the U.S. labor market. The fundamental problem with the bill was that its architects ignored the *future* labor needs of U.S. employers. After the amnesty took effect, our economy continued to grow and attract more foreign workers. But since the legal channels available were not sufficiently expanded, migrants once again began coming illegally, which is how today's undocumented population grew to its current size. Another amnesty, by itself, will do no more to "solve" the problem in the long run than the first one did.

It's unfortunate that the "no amnesty" crowd has been able to suck up so much oxygen in this debate. Immigration hysterics on talk radio and cable news have used the term effectively to end conversations. And restrictionists in Congress have used it as a political slogan to block reform. But from a public policy perspective, the fate of the 12 million illegals already here is largely a side issue, a problem that will solve itself over time if we get the other reforms right.

As in 1986, our economy and society have already absorbed most of these illegal workers. Many have married Americans, started families, bought homes, laid down roots. If their presence here is a problem, it is a self-correcting one. In time, they will grow old and pass on with the rest of us. The Obama administration would do better to focus less on whether to grant amnesty or to deport them and more on how to stop feeding their numbers going forward.

---

*Expanding legal immigration ought to be where the Obama administration channels its energies.*

---

## Expanding Legal Immigration

Unfortunately, the president will be pressed to do the opposite. The nation's two largest labor groups, the AFL-CIO [American Federation of Labor and Congress of Industrial Organizations] and Change to Win, have already announced that they will oppose any new guest worker initiatives and any significant expansion of temporary work programs already in place. Democrats and advocacy groups, who tend to see immigration as a humanitarian issue more than an economic one, will likely side with labor. But history suggests that such programs are effective in reducing illegal entries. Past experience shows that economic migrants have no desire to be here illegally. They will use the front door if it's available to them, which reduces pressure on the border and frees up homeland security resources to target drug dealers, gang members, potential terrorists, and other real threats.

Nearly seven decades ago, the United States faced labor shortages in agriculture stemming from World War II, and growers turned to the [Franklin D.] Roosevelt administration for help. The result was the Bracero Program, which allowed hundreds of thousands of Mexican farm workers to enter the country legally as seasonal laborers. In place from 1942 to 1964, the program was jointly operated by the departments of Justice, State and Labor. As the program was expanded after World War II to meet the labor needs of a growing U.S. economy, illegal border crossings fell by 95%. A 1980 Congressional Research Service report concluded that "without question," the program was "instrumental in ending the illegal alien problem of the mid-1940s and 1950s." Apparently, the law of supply and demand doesn't stop at the Rio Grande.

Beginning in 1960, the program was phased out after it faced opposition from labor unions. And since nothing comparable emerged to replace it, illegal entries began to rise again. The point isn't that we need to resurrect the Bracero Program, or that guest worker programs alone will stop illegal immigration from Mexico. But a Bracero-like program with the proper worker protections ought to be the template. And expanding legal immigration ought to be where the Obama administration channels its energies.

Granted, this will be a hard sell at a time when growing numbers of Americans are out of work. Even in good times, zero-sum thinking—the notion that what is gained by some must be lost by others—dominates discussions about immigrants and jobs. But the schooling and skills that the typical Mexican immigrant brings to the U.S. labor market differ markedly from the typical American's, which is why the two don't tend to compete with each other for employment. Labor economists like Richard Vedder have documented that, historically, higher levels of immigration to the United States are associated with lower levels of unemployment. Immigrants are catalysts for economic growth, not job-stealers.

There are plenty of ways and plenty of time to deal with the country's undocumented millions in a fair and humane manner. But we'd do better to focus first on not adding to their numbers. If the fate of this group instead drives the policy discussion, we're more likely to end up with the status quo or faux reforms like amnesty that dodge the real problem. By all means, Mr. Obama, lead the fight for immigration reform. But don't lead with your chin.

# Immigration Reform Must Contain a Temporary Worker Program

*Daniel Griswold*

*Daniel Griswold is director of the Center for Trade Policy Studies at the Cato Institute, a conservative think tank.*

Prospects for comprehensive immigration reform are on the rise. Voters in November [2006] replaced the GOP Congress with Democratic leadership that has shown itself to be more open to expanding legal channels for immigrant workers. Nonetheless, momentum is building for major reform—and not a minute too soon. In testimony before the Senate Judiciary Committee on March 1 [2007], Commerce Secretary Carlos Gutierrez remarked that America's dynamic economy continues to create jobs for low-skilled workers as well as higher-skilled ones, yet the number of Americans willing to fill lower-end jobs continues to shrink.

---

*Immigration reform must contain a workable temporary worker program.*

---

## Expanding Temporary Visas

From 1996 to 2004, the number of adult Americans without a high school education—the demographic group that typically fills low-skilled jobs—fell by 4.6 million. The biggest flaw in our immigration system is its lack of a sufficient legal channel for low-skilled immigrants who are crucial to filling that gap between demand and supply on the lower rungs of the labor ladder.

In the face of those powerful economic and demographic trends, federal enforcement efforts have failed to stem the inflow of low-skilled immigrants. Secretary of Homeland Security Michael Chertoff, after reporting the administration's increased efforts at border enforcement, told the committee that a policy of enforcement-only cannot work. He called on Congress to create a temporary worker program so that foreign workers can enter legally to fill jobs that U.S. workers do not want.

"This regulated channel for temporary workers would dramatically reduce the pressure on our borders, aid our economy and ease the task of our law enforcement agents inside the country," Chertoff told the committee. "There is an inextricable link between the creation of a temporary worker program and better enforcement at the border."

The last major effort to stop illegal immigration was the Immigration Reform and Control Act of 1986. It failed because it lacked any expansion of legal immigration to meet U.S. labor needs. It legalized 2.7 million immigrants and ramped up enforcement, but with no allowance for the entry of new, legal workers, the population of illegal immigrants soon began its inevitable increase to the current level of an estimated 12 million.

Immigration reform must contain a workable temporary worker program. Such a program must create a sufficient number of visas to meet the needs of the U.S. economy. A crucial flaw in the McCain-Kennedy bill passed by the Senate last May [2006] was that it capped annual visas at 200,000—far below actual demand.

---

*True reforms must also avoid stifling labor regulations that discourage legal hiring.*

---

According to Labor Department projections, our economy will continue to create a net 400,000 or more low-skilled jobs annually in service sectors such as food preparation, cleaning, construction, landscaping and retail. A visa cap below the actual demand in our economy would only perpetuate the problem of illegal immigration.

## Other Necessary Reforms

True reforms must also avoid stifling labor regulations that discourage legal hiring. Union leaders are pressuring Democrats to require that temporary workers be paid "prevailing wages"—that is, artificially high, union-level wages rather than market wages. This would be a recipe for failure, because many of the jobs filled by immigrant workers are low-skilled, low-wage jobs that would simply not exist in the legal economy if union-level wages were mandated.

Adding cumbersome labor rules would only perpetuate the underground labor market created by the current system.

Finally, any reform worthy of the name must offer a path to legalization for the millions of undocumented workers already here. Deporting them all would be impractical, yet continuing indefinitely with millions living in a legal twilight zone also is unacceptable.

Waiting won't make the problem go away. If the new Congress fails to enact comprehensive immigration reform, the alternative will be two more years of widespread illegal immigration, and no one but the smugglers at the border will benefit by it.

# Immigration Policy Should Be Overhauled to Take National Identity Seriously

*Amy Chua*

*Amy Chua is a professor at Yale Law School and the author of* Day of Empire: How Hyperpowers Rise to Global Dominance—and Why They Fall *and* World on Fire: How Exporting Free Market Democracy Breeds Ethnic Hatred and Global Instability.

If you don't speak Spanish, Miami really can feel like a foreign country. In any restaurant, the conversation at the next table is more likely to be in Spanish than English. And Miami's population is only 65 percent Hispanic. El Paso is 76 percent Latino. Flushing, N.Y., is 60 percent immigrant, mainly Chinese.

Chinatowns and Little Italys have long been part of America's urban landscape, but would it be all right to have entire U.S. cities where most people spoke and did business in Chinese, Spanish or even Arabic? Are too many third world, non-English-speaking immigrants destroying our national identity?

For some Americans, even asking such questions is racist. At the other end of the spectrum, conservative talk show host Bill O'Reilly fulminates against floods of immigrants who threaten to change America's "complexion" and replace what he calls the "white, Christian, male power structure."

But for the large majority in between, Democrats and Republicans alike, these questions are painful, and there are no easy answers. At some level, most of us cherish our legacy as a nation of immigrants. But are all immigrants really equally likely to make good Americans? Are we, as [political scientist] Samuel Huntington warns, in danger of losing our core values and devolving "into a loose confederation of ethnic, racial, cultural and political groups, with little or nothing in common apart from their location in the territory of what had been the United States of America"?

My parents arrived in the United States in 1961, so poor that they couldn't afford heat their first winter. I grew up speaking only Chinese at home (for every English word accidentally uttered, my sister and I got one whack of the chopsticks). Today, my father is a professor at Berkeley, and I'm a professor at Yale Law School. As the daughter of immigrants, a grateful beneficiary of America's tolerance and opportunity, I could not be more pro-immigrant.

Nevertheless, I think Huntington has a point.

## Dangers of Disintegration

Around the world today, nations face violence and instability as a result of their increasing pluralism and diversity. Across Europe, immigration has resulted in unassimilated, largely Muslim enclaves that are hotbeds of unrest and even terrorism. The riots in France late last year [2007] were just the latest manifestation. With Muslims poised to become a majority in Amsterdam and elsewhere within a decade, major west European cities could undergo a profound transformation. Not surprisingly, virulent anti-immigration parties are on the rise.

---

*The United States . . . has been . . . successful, at least since the Civil War, in forging a national identity strong enough to hold together its widely divergent communities.*

---

Not long ago, Czechoslovakia, Yugoslavia and the Soviet Union disintegrated when their national identities proved too weak to bind together diverse peoples. Iraq is the latest example of how crucial national identity is. So far, it has found no overarching identity strong enough to unite its Kurds, Shiites and Sunnis.

The United States is in no danger of imminent disintegration. But this is because it has been so successful, at least since the Civil War, in forging a national identity strong enough to hold together its widely divergent communities. We should not take this unifying identity for granted.

The greatest empire in history, ancient Rome, collapsed when its cultural and political glue dissolved, and peoples who had long thought of themselves as Romans turned against the empire. In part, this fragmentation occurred because of a massive influx of immigrants from a very different culture. The "barbarians" who sacked Rome were Germanic immigrants who never fully assimilated.

Does this mean that it's time for the United States to shut its borders and reassert its "white, Christian" identity and what Huntington calls its Anglo-Saxon, Protestant "core values"?

## Anti-Immigrant Mistakes

No. The anti-immigration camp makes at least two critical mistakes.

First, it neglects the indispensable role that immigrants have played in building American wealth and power. In the 19th century, the United States would never have become an industrial and agricultural powerhouse without the millions of poor Irish, Polish, Italian and other newcomers who mined coal, laid rail and milled steel. European immigrants led to the United States winning the race for the atomic bomb.

Today, American leadership in the Digital Revolution—so central to our military and economic preeminence—owes an enormous debt to immigrant contributions. Andrew Grove (cofounder of Intel), Vinod Khosla (Sun Microsystems) and Sergey Brin (Google) are immigrants. Between 1995 and 2005,

52.4 percent of Silicon Valley start-ups had one key immigrant founder. And Vikram S. Pandit's recent appointment to the helm of Citigroup means that 14 CEOs of Fortune 100 companies are foreign-born.

---

*Immigration advocates are too often guilty of an uncritical political correctness that avoids hard questions about national identity and imposes no obligations on immigrants.*

---

The United States is in a fierce global competition to attract the world's best high-tech scientists and engineers—most of whom are not white Christians. Just this past summer [2007], Microsoft opened a large new software-development center in Canada, in part because of the difficulty of obtaining U.S. visas for foreign engineers.

Second, anti-immigration talking heads forget that their own scapegoating vitriol will, if anything, drive immigrants further from the U.S. mainstream. One reason we don't have Europe's enclaves is our unique success in forging an ethnically and religiously neutral national identity, uniting individuals of all backgrounds. This is America's glue, and people like Huntington and O'Reilly unwittingly imperil it.

Nevertheless, immigration naysayers also have a point.

America's glue can be subverted by too much tolerance. Immigration advocates are too often guilty of an uncritical political correctness that avoids hard questions about national identity and imposes no obligations on immigrants. For these well-meaning idealists, there is no such thing as too much diversity.

## Maintaining Our Heritage

The right thing for the United States to do—and the best way to keep Americans in favor of immigration—is to take national identity seriously while maintaining our heritage as a land of opportunity. U.S. immigration policy should be tolerant but also tough. Here are five suggestions:

---

*Apart from nuclear families (spouse, minor children, possibly parents), the special preference for family members should be drastically reduced.*

---

*Overhaul admission priorities.* Since 1965, the chief admission criterion has been family reunification. This was a welcome replacement for the ethnically discriminatory quota system that preceded it. But once the brothers and sisters of a current U.S. resident get in, they can sponsor their own extended families. In 2006, more than 800,000 immigrants were admitted on this basis. By contrast, only about 70,000 immigrants were admitted on the basis of employment skills, with an additional 65,000 temporary visas granted to highly skilled workers.

This is backward. Apart from nuclear families (spouse, minor children, possibly parents), the special preference for family members should be drastically reduced. As soon as my father got citizenship, his relatives in the Philippines asked him to sponsor them. Soon, his mother, brother, sister and sister-in-law were also U.S. citizens or permanent residents. This was nice for my family, but frankly there is nothing especially fair about it.

Instead, the immigration system should reward ability and be keyed to the country's labor needs, skilled or unskilled, technological or agricultural. In particular, we should significantly increase the number of visas for highly skilled workers, putting them on a fast track for citizenship.

*Make English the official national language.* A common language is critical to cohesion and national identity in an ethnically diverse society. Americans of all backgrounds should be encouraged to speak more languages—I've forced my own daughters to learn Mandarin (minus the threat of chopsticks)—but offering Spanish-language public education to Spanish-speaking children is the wrong kind of indulgence. Native-language education should be overhauled, and more stringent English proficiency requirements for citizenship should be set up.

*Immigrants must embrace the nation's civic virtues.* It took my parents years to see the importance of participating in the larger community. When I was in third grade, my mother signed me up for Girl Scouts. I think she liked the uniforms and merit badges, but when I told her that I was picking up trash and visiting soup kitchens, she was horrified.

For many immigrants, only family matters. Even when immigrants get involved in politics, they often focus on protecting their own and protesting discrimination. That they can do so is one of the great virtues of U.S. democracy. But a mindset based solely on taking care of your own factionalizes our society.

---

*We need to enforce the law against not only illegal aliens, but also against those who hire them.*

---

Like all Americans, immigrants have a responsibility to contribute to the social fabric. It's up to each immigrant community to fight off an "enclave" mentality and give back to their new country. It's not healthy for Chinese to hire only Chinese, or Koreans only Koreans. By contrast, the free health clinic set up by Muslim Americans in Los Angeles—serving the entire poor community—is a model to emulate. Immigrants are integrated at the moment they realize that their success is intertwined with everyone else's.

*Enforce the law.* Illegal immigration, along with terrorism, is the chief cause of today's anti-immigration backlash. It is also inconsistent with the rule of law, which, as any immigrant from a developing country will tell you, is a critical aspect of U.S. identity. But if we're serious about this problem, we need to enforce the law against not only illegal aliens, but also against those who hire them.

It's the worst of all worlds to allow U.S. employers who hire illegal aliens—thus keeping the flow of illegal workers coming—to break the law while demonizing the aliens as law-breakers. An Arizona law that took effect Jan. 1 [2007] tightens the screws on employers who hire undocumented workers, but this issue can't be left up to a single state.

*Make the United States an equal-opportunity immigration magnet.* That the 11 million to 20 million illegal immigrants are 80 percent Mexican and Central American is itself a problem. This is emphatically not for the reason Huntington gives—that Hispanics supposedly don't share America's core values. But if the U.S. immigration system is to reflect and further our ethnically neutral identity, it must itself be ethnically neutral, offering equal opportunity to Sudanese, Estonians, Burmese and so on. The starkly disproportionate ratio of Latinos—reflecting geographical fortuity and a large measure of lawbreaking—is inconsistent with this principle.

Immigrants who turn their backs on American values don't deserve to be here. But those of us who turn our backs on immigrants misunderstand the secret of America's success and what it means to be American.

# The Barack Obama Administration Should De-emphasize the Link Between Illegal Immigrants and Terrorists

*Tom Barry*

*Tom Barry is a senior analyst at the Center for International Policy, a policy research organization, where he directs the Trans-Border Project of the Americas Policy Program.*

The terrorist attacks of Sept. 11 [2001] drastically altered the traditional political economy of immigration. The millions of undocumented immigrants—those who crossed the border illegally or overstayed their visas—who were living and working in the United States were no longer simply regarded as a shadow population or as surplus cheap labor. In the public and policy debate, immigrants were increasingly defined as threats to the nation's security. Categorizing immigrants as national security threats gave the government's flailing immigration law enforcement and border control operations a new unifying logic that has propelled the immigrant crackdown forward.

Responsibility for immigration law enforcement and border control passed from the Justice Department [DOJ] to the new Department of Homeland Security (DHS). In Congress Democrats and Republicans alike readily supported a vast expansion of the country's immigration control apparatus—doubling the number of border patrol agents and authorizing a tripling of immigrant prison beds.

Today, after the shift in the immigration debate, the $15 billion-plus DHS budget for immigration affairs has fueled an

Tom Barry, "The New Political Economy of Immigration," *Dollars & Sense*, January-February 2009. Copyright © 2009 Economic Affairs Bureau, Inc. Reproduced by permission of Dollars & Sense, a progressive economics magazine. www.dollarsandsense.org.

immigrant-crackdown economy that has greatly boosted the already-bloated prison industry. Even now [2009], with the economy imploding, immigrants are currently behind one of the country's most profitable industries: they are the nation's fastest growing sector of the U.S. prison population.

Across the country new prisons are hurriedly being constructed to house the hundreds of thousands of immigrants caught each year. State and local governments are vying with each other to attract new immigrant prisons as the foundation of their rural "economic development" plans.

---

*While the increased numbers of immigrants being arrested, imprisoned, and deported certainly demonstrate that DHS is busy, they don't demonstrate that DHS is stopping terrorism.*

---

While DHS is driving immigrants from their jobs and homes, U.S. firms in the business of providing prison beds are raking in record profits from the immigrant crackdown. Although only one piece of the broader story of immigration, it's all a part of the new political economy of immigration.

## Dangerous People

In the new national security context, undocumented immigrants are not just outlaws: They are "dangerous people" who threaten the homeland.

The two DHS agencies involved in immigration enforcement—Immigration and Customs Enforcement (ICE) and Customs and Border Protection (CBP)—have seen their funds increased disproportionately over the last several years, doubling in size while total DHS funding has increased by just a third. The funding for these two agencies is set to rise 19.1% in 2009 while the overall DHS budget will increase by only 6.8%. Hunting down immigrants has become a top DHS priority. As, DHS says its mission is "to prevent terrorist attacks against the nation and to protect our nation from dangerous people."

Immigrants caught up in DHS dragnets, work site enforcement raids, and border patrols were the "metrics of success" that DHS secretary Michael Chertoff pointed to in his July 18, 2008 congressional testimony. He used the dramatically increased number of immigrant apprehensions and "removals" as metrics to show that DHS is succeeding in its goal to "secure the homeland and protect the American people."

While the increased numbers of immigrants being arrested, imprisoned, and deported certainly demonstrate that DHS is busy, they don't demonstrate that DHS is stopping terrorism. Never in its congressional testimonies or media releases does DHS present evidence that shows how the number of immigrants captured improves national security.

A 2007 study by the Transactional Records Access Clearinghouse (TRAC) at Syracuse University found that there has been no increase in terrorism or national security charges against immigrants since 2001. In fact, despite the increased enforcement operations by Homeland Security, more immigrants were charged annually in immigration courts with national security or terrorism-related offenses in a three-year period in the mid-1990s (1994–96) than in a comparable period (2004–2006) since Sept. 11 [2001]. According to the TRAC study, "A decade later, national security charges were brought against 114 individuals, down about a third. Meanwhile for the same period, terrorism charges are down more than three-fourths, to just 12."

## Enforcing the "Rule of Law"

Rather than addressing immigration as the complex socioeconomic issue that it is, Homeland Security has reduced immigration policy to a system of crime and punishment. Applying the simplistic law-and-order logic propagated by restrictionists, DHS regards undocumented immigrants not as workers, community members, and parents but as criminals.

---

*Eager to cash in on immigrant detention, private prison firms and local governments are rushing to supply [the government] . . . with the prisons needed to house . . . immigrants.*

---

Following the lead of the anti-immigration institutes and right-wing think tanks, Chertoff came to Homeland Security with a new interpretation of the department's immigration law enforcement and border control operations: Commitment to a strict enforcement regime to protect the country against foreign terrorists, and to reassert the "rule of law."

In the aftermath of Sept. 11 [2001], the restrictionist camp found that their messaging about the "illegality" and "criminality" of undocumented immigrants took on a new resonance. They proceeded to upscale their "what don't you understand about illegal?" message, to a more conceptual framing of undocumented immigration. Undocumented immigrants now represented a threat to the "rule of law" inside a nation that had just come under foreign attack by foreign outlaws.

Their new language about immigration policy started popping up everywhere, from the pronouncements of immigrants' rights groups to the Democratic Party platform. Instead of promising an "earned path to citizenship," as it has in the past, the party stated that undocumented immigrants will be required to "get right with the law."

Looking ahead, Janet Napolitano, President [Barack] Obama's nominee to replace Chertoff, while no anti-immigration hardliner, still seems poised to adopt the same law-and-order logic. As a lawyer, former federal prosecutor, and a governor who has insisted on more border control and stood behind a tough employer-sanctions law, Napolitano can be expected to follow the lead of Chertoff and the Democratic

Party in insisting that current immigration laws be strictly enforced "to reassert the rule of law."

## Immigrants Mean Business

Political imperatives—protecting the homeland and enforcing the "rule of law"—have over the past eight years countervailed against the economic forces that have historically led in setting immigration policy. Although the immigrant labor market persists, the increased risks for both employer and worker, along with the recessionary economy, appear to be exercising downward pressure on both supply and demand.

But even in the flagging economy, the immigrant crackdown has invigorated other market forces. Eager to cash in on immigrant detention, private prison firms and local governments are rushing to supply Homeland Security and the Justice Department with the prisons needed to house the hundreds of thousands of immigrants captured by ICE and border patrol agents.

In the prison industry, "bed" is a euphemism for a place behind bars. Even President [George W.] Bush talked the prison bed language when discussing immigration policy. When visiting the Rio Grande Valley in south Texas in 2006 to promote the immigrant crackdown, the president said: "Beds are our number one priority."

The number of beds for detained immigrants in DHS centers has increased by more than a third since 2002. There are now 32,000 beds available for the revolving population of immigrants on the path to deportation, and another 1,000 are scheduled to come on line in 2009. This doesn't include beds for immigrants in Homeland Security custody that are provided by county, state, and the Federal Bureau of Prisons [BOP].

At the insistence of such immigration restrictionists as Rep. Tom Tancredo (R-Colo.), the Intelligence Reform and Terrorism Prevention Act of 2004 contained an authorization for an additional 40,000 beds to accommodate immigrants under U.S. government custody.

At the onset of the immigration crackdown two years ago, ICE dubbed its promise to find a detention center or prison bed for all arrested immigrants "Operation Reservation Guaranteed." The Justice Department has a similar initiative to ensure that the U.S. Marshals Service has beds available for detainees—about 180,000 a year, of whom more than 30% are held on immigration charges.

Most of the prison beds contracted by ICE and DOJ's Office of the Federal Detention Trustee are with local governments; ICE has more than 300 intergovernmental agreements with county and city governments to hold immigrants, while DOJ has some 1,200 such agreements. In many cases, particularly with contracts for hundreds of prison beds, the local government then subcontracts with a private prison company to operate the facility.

Prison beds translate into per diem [by the day] payments from the federal government that are well above the hotel room rates in the remote rural communities where most of these immigrant prisons are located. With these per diems running from $70 to $95 for each immigrant imprisoned, local governments and private firms are hurrying to expand existing facilities or to create new ones. . . .

## New Political Economy of Immigration

What started off as a war against terrorism has devolved into a war against immigrants. The current "enforcement-only" approach to immigration policy has created a morass of new problems, including a host of human rights and financial issues associated with the annual detention and removal of immigrants. The immigrant crackdown has given rise to an unregulated complex of jails, detention centers, and prisons that create profit from the immigrant crackdown.

At the outset of a new administration and new era, the political economy of immigration is decidedly anti-immigrant. Political and economic factors have combined to create a harsh environment for undocumented immigrants, present and future. Immigration reform may not be a top priority, but the Obama administration and new Congress would do well to begin to address the challenge of reshaping the political economy of immigration.

First steps could include a more careful articulation of the intersection of immigration, rule of law, and national security. Napolitano should explain that the real threat to the rule of law is not having an immigration policy that provides a legal pathway to integration for the 11 million immigrants already within the United States.

What's more, she would do well to disarticulate the links established by the Bush administration between immigrants and terrorists. At the same time, closer links must be made between immigration policy and economic policy, guarding against labor exploitation while considering domestic economic need.

Instead of a policy based on a calm assessment of the costs and benefits of immigrant labor to the U.S. economy, current immigration policy has been hijacked by the politics of fear, resentment, scapegoating, and nativism. The "enforcement only" immigration policy has fostered a national immigrant prison complex that feeds on ever-increasing numbers of arrested immigrants. As county commissioner Ernie Chapa said, "Any time the numbers are high, it's good for the county because it brings more income."

# Congress Should Pass Comprehensive Immigration Reform

*Simon Rosenberg*

*Simon Rosenberg is a political strategist and the founder of the New Democrat Network, a U.S. political group that promotes progressive Democratic candidates.*

Today [April 30, 2009] in the Senate, Senator [Charles] Schumer is holding an important hearing: "Comprehensive Immigration Reform in 2009, Can We Do It and How?" At NDN [New Democrat Network, a Washington-based think tank], we believe the answer to whether Congress can pass reform this year is "yes." Below are seven reasons why:

1) *In tough economic times, we need to remove the "trap door" under the minimum wage.*

One of the first acts of the new Democratic Congress back in 2007 was to raise the minimum wage, to help alleviate the downward pressure on wages we had seen throughout the decade even prior to the current Great Recession. The problem with this strategy is that the minimum wage and other worker protections required by American law do not extend to those workers here illegally. With economic times worsening here and in the home countries of the migrants, unscrupulous employers have much more leverage over, and incentive to keep, undocumented workers. With five percent of the current workforce—amazingly, with one out of every 20 workers now undocumented, this situation creates an unacceptable race to the bottom, downward pressure on wages, at a time when we need to be doing more for those struggling to get by, not less.

Legalizing the five percent of the work force that is un-documented would create a higher wage and benefit floor than exists today for all workers, further helping, as was intended by the increase in the minimum wage two years ago, to alleviate the downward pressure on wages for those struggling the most in this tough economy.

---

*Legalization does not create a flood of new immigrants—... it puts the immigrant worker on a more even playing field with legal American workers.*

---

Additionally, it needs to be understood that these undocumenteds are already here and working. If you are undocumented, you are not eligible for welfare. If you are not working, you go home. Thus, in order to remove this "trap door," we need to either kick five percent of [the] existing American workforce out of the country—a moral and economic impossibility—or legalize them. There is no third way on this one. They stay and become citizens or we chase them away.

Finally, what you hear from some of the opponents of immigration reform is that by passing reform, all of these immigrants will come and take the jobs away of everyday Americans. But again, the undocumented immigrants are already here, working, having kids, supporting local businesses. Legalization does not create a flood of new immigrants—in fact, as discussed earlier, it puts the immigrant worker on a more even playing field with legal American workers. It does the very inverse of what is being suggested—it creates fairer competition for American workers—not unfair competition. The status quo is what should be most unacceptable to those who claim they are advocating for the American worker.

2) *In a time of tight budgets, passing immigration reform will bring more money into the federal treasury.*

Putting the undocumented population on the road to citizenship will also increase tax revenue in a time of economic crisis, as the newly legal immigrants will pay fees and fines, and become fully integrated into the U.S. tax-paying system. When immigration reform legislation passed the Senate in 2006, the Congressional Budget Office estimate that accompanied the bill projected treasury revenues would see a net increase of $44 billion over 10 years.

3) *Reforming our immigration system will increasingly be seen as a critical part of any comprehensive strategy to calm the increasingly violent border region.*

Tackling the growing influence of the drug cartels in Mexico is going to be hard, cost a great deal of money, and take a long time. One quick and early step toward calming the region will be to take decisive action on clearing up one piece of the problem—the vast illegal trade in undocumented migrants. Legalization will also help give these millions of families a greater stake in the United States, which will make it less likely that they contribute to the spread of the cartels' influence.

4) *Fixing the immigration system will help reinforce that it is a "new day" for U.S.-Latin American relations.*

To his credit, President [Barack] Obama has made it clear that he wants to see a significant improvement in our relations with our Latin neighbors and very clearly communicated that message during his recent trips to Mexico and the Summit of the Americas. Just as offering a new policy toward Cuba is part of establishing that it is truly a "new day" in hemispheric relations, ending the shameful treatment of Latin migrants here in the United States will go a long way in signaling that America is taking its relations with its southern neighbors much more seriously than in the past.

5) *Passing immigration reform this year clears the way for a clean census next year.*

Even though the government is constitutionally required to count everyone living in the United States every 10 years, the national GOP has made it clear that it will block efforts for the Census Bureau to count undocumented immigrants. Conducting a clean and thorough census is hard in any environment. If we add a protracted legal and political battle on top—think Norm Coleman [a former Republican senator from Minnesota whose 2008 reelection race with Democrat Al Franken was disputed for many months], a politicized U.S. Attorney process, *Bush v. Gore* [a case involving the winner of the 2004 presidential election that was decided by the Supreme Court]—the chance of a failed or flawed census rises dramatically. This of course would not be good for the nation.

Passing immigration reform this year would go a long way to ensuring we have a clean and effective census count next year.

6) *The administration and Congress will grow weary of what we call "immigration proxy wars," and will want the issue taken off the table.*

---

*Immigration reform ... would [reduce] ... what is the most virulent form of racism in American society today—the attacks on Hispanics and undocumented immigrants.*

---

With rising violence in Mexico, and the everyday drumbeat of clashes and conflicts over immigration in communities across America, the broken immigration system is not going to fade from public consciousness any time soon. The very vocal minority on the right—those who put this issue on the table in the first place—will continue to try to attach amendments to other bills ensuring that various government benefits are not conferred upon undocumenteds. We have already seen battles pop up this year on virtually every major bill Congress has taken up, including SCHIP [State Children's Health Insurance Program] and the stimulus. By the fall [2009], I think leaders of both parties will grow weary of these proxy battles popping up on every issue and will want to resolve the issue once and for all. Passing immigration reform will become essential to making progress on other much needed societal goals like moving toward universal health insurance.

7) *Finally, in the age of Obama, we must be vigilant to stamp out racism wherever it appears.*

Passing immigration reform this year would help take the air out of the balloon of what is the most virulent form of racism in American society today—the attacks on Hispanics and undocumented immigrants. It will be increasingly difficult for the president and his allies to somehow argue that watching [radio and television show host] Glenn Beck act out the burning alive of a person on the air over immigration, "left leaning" Ed Schultz give air time to avowed racist Tom Tancredo on MSNBC, or Republican ads comparing Mexican immigrants to Islamic terrorists is somehow different from the racially insensitive speech that got Rush Limbaugh kicked off *Monday Night Football,* or Don Imus kicked off the radio.

So for those of us who want to see this vexing national problem addressed this year, this important hearing is a critical step forward. But we still have a long way to go, and a lot of work ahead of us if we are to get this done this year.

# The Barack Obama Administration Should Forget About Comprehensive Immigration Reform and Push Reforms One Step at a Time

## Errol Louis

*Errol Louis is a columnist for the* New York Daily News, *a New York newspaper. He also hosts a radio program on WWRL in New York.*

President [Barack] Obama's regrettable pledge to enact comprehensive immigration reform suggests he will repeat the mistaken attempt of Washington leaders to craft an all-in-one solution to the wildly different strands of our tangled immigration knot.

It's as if the White House brain trust has learned nothing from recent legislative history. Comprehensive bills failed in 2005, 2006 and 2007, first during a Republican-led Congress and later under Democratic leadership.

The last three plans crashed and burned because each contained too many complex, controversial moving parts. It would have been tough enough to get agreement on how to secure our porous southwestern border, but lawmakers combined border enforcement with schemes to offer a path to citizenship for America's estimated 12 million illegal immigrants, an idea that always provokes a roar of opposition from those who see amnesty as rewarding criminal behavior.

To this already combustible mix, earlier failed bills added gasoline: proposals to expand work visas and create guest worker programs.

The result, over and over, has been a political minefield that blew up every bill, leaving a system that's still broken.

Small wonder that White House Chief of Staff Rahm Emanuel, who had a front-row view of the legislative gridlock as a member of Congress, once said that immigration would be a high priority for the *second* term of the Obama administration.

He was on to something.

---

*[President Barack] Obama should start [immigration reform] by picking two pieces of low-hanging fruit: tighter border security and sensible curbs on immigrant-hunting raids.*

---

## One Step at a Time

Instead of putting immigration reform on hold until every last volatile element can be resolved in a grand bargain, Obama should start by picking two pieces of low-hanging fruit: tighter border security and sensible curbs on immigrant-hunting raids.

Opinion polls and common sense suggest that no immigration reform policy will have credibility until we end the chaos on the southwest border, where drug smuggling cartels are in a shooting war that has killed thousands—including 200 Americans—since 2004, with murders in Mexico now ticking up to a rate of 250 a month.

If Obama, working closely with Mexican officials, manages to tamp down the violence, he'll earn political capital needed to convince border state officials to venture down the politically treacherous road to discussing pathways to citizenship and looser work visa rules.

An even faster way to create political common ground would be to inject some sanity into the current immigrant-hunting frenzy that has led federal and local law enforcement agencies to seize, and detain, hundreds of *American citizens*—some of whom have even been mistakenly deported.

---

*We can build national consensus to create a better, fairer immigration system. But it has to happen one step at a time.*

---

Nobody keeps track of the numbers, but the evidence suggests the practice is widespread. A recently published investigation by the Associated Press confirmed 55 cases of Americans locked up or removed from the country over the last eight years, including one Brooklyn man imprisoned for nine years until a U.S. court declared him a citizen.

A single immigrant rights group in Arizona testified to Congress of seeing 40 to 50 cases each month of jailed people with citizenship claims. In 2007, the Vera Institute of Justice, a prison reform group, discovered 322 detainees with citizenship claims behind bars.

The nation, it seems, has gone nuts over illegal immigrants. We will deport an estimated 400,000 people this year, a number that rises to 1 million if you add those who will simply take off rather than face penalties like imprisonment or a permanent ban. Yet many continue to argue that the country isn't doing enough to catch and deport illegals.

We can build national consensus to create a better, fairer immigration system. But it has to happen one step at a time.

# Organizations to Contact

*The editors have compiled the following list of organizations concerned with the issues debated in this book. The descriptions are derived from materials provided by the organizations. All have publications or information available for interested readers. The list was compiled on the date of publication of the present volume; the information provided here may change. Be aware that many organizations take several weeks or longer to respond to inquiries, so allow as much time as possible.*

**American Civil Liberties Union (ACLU)**
125 Broad Street, 18th Floor, New York, NY 10004
(212) 549-2500
Web site: www.aclu.org

The American Civil Liberties Union (ACLU) is a national organization that champions the rights found in the Declaration of Independence and the U.S. Constitution. The ACLU Immigrants' Rights Project advocates for the rights of immigrants, refugees, and noncitizens. The project has published various reports and position papers, including *Worlds Apart: How Deporting Immigrants After 9/11 Tore Families Apart and Shattered Communities* and *America's Disappeared: Seeking International Justice for Immigrants Detained After September 11.*

**Americans for Immigration Control (AIC)**
PO Box 738, Monterey, VA 24465
(540) 468-2023 • fax: (540) 468-2026
e-mail: aic@immigrationcontrol.com
Web site: www.immigrationcontrol.com

Americans for Immigration Control (AIC) is a lobbying organization that works to influence Congress to adopt legal reforms to reduce U.S. immigration. It supports increased funding for the U.S. Customs and Border Protection, sanctions against employers who hire illegal immigrants, termination of all public assistance except emergency medical for illegal immigrants, and reduction of all immigration to levels of 250,000 per year. AIC's Web site contains information about immigration, including a blog and lists of books and publications.

### American Friends Service Committee (AFSC)

1501 Cherry Street, Philadelphia, PA   19102
(215) 241-7000 • fax: (215) 241-7275
e-mail: afscinfo@afsc.org
Web site: www.afsc.org

The American Friends Service Committee (AFSC) is a Quaker organization that carries out service, social justice, and peace programs throughout the world. An AFSC initiative called Project Voice helps pro-immigrant organizations lobby for pro-immigrant national immigration policies and immigrants' rights. The AFSC Web site contains news updates, brochures, statements, and press releases relating to illegal immigration.

### American Immigration Council

1331 G Street NW, Suite 200, Washington, DC   20005
(202) 507-7500 • fax: (202) 742-5619
Web site: www.americanimmigrationcouncil.org

The American Immigration Council is a tax-exempt, not-for-profit, educational, charitable organization that works to improve public understanding of immigration law and policy and the value of immigration to American society. Its Immigration Policy Center (IPC) conducts research and analysis about the contributions made to America by immigrants and works to educate and influence the public and policy makers to promote immigrants' rights. The IPC publishes numerous publications on immigration topics.

### California Coalition for Immigration Reform (CCIR)

Box 2744-117, Huntington Beach, CA   92649
(714) 665-2500 • fax: (714) 846-9682

e-mail: barb@ccir.net
Web site: www.ccir.net

The California Coalition for Immigration Reform (CCIR) is a grassroots volunteer organization representing Americans concerned with illegal immigration. CCIR seeks to educate and inform the public and to effectively ensure enforcement of the nation's immigration laws. CCIR produces alerts, bulletins, videos, bumper stickers, other immigration-related products, and an immigration blog.

## Cato Institute

1000 Massachusetts Avenue NW
Washington, DC   20001-5403
(202) 842-0200 • fax: (202) 842-3490
Web site: www.cato.org

The Cato Institute is a libertarian public policy research foundation dedicated to stimulating policy debate. It believes immigration is good for the U.S. economy and favors easing immigration restrictions. Its Web site contains various articles on illegal immigration, including "Electronic Employment Eligibility Verification: Franz Kafka's Solution to Illegal Immigration" and "Backfire at the Border: Why Enforcement Without Legalization."

## Center for Immigration Studies (CIS)

1522 K Street NW, Suite 820, Washington, DC   20005-1202
(202) 466-8185 • fax: (202) 466-8076
e-mail: center@cis.org
Web site: www.cis.org

The Center for Immigration Studies (CIS) is an independent, nonpartisan think tank devoted to research and policy analysis of the economic, social, demographic, fiscal, and other impacts of immigration on the United States. CIS's Web site contains background papers, reports, other publications, and a blog relevant to the immigration debate. Recent examples of CIS publications include *Immigrant Unemployment at Record High* and *Immigration Enforcement in Meatpacking.*

## Essential Worker Immigration Coalition (EWIC)

1615 H Street NW, Washington, DC 20062
(202) 463-5931
Web site: www.ewic.org

The Essential Worker Immigration Coalition (EWIC) is a coalition of businesses, trade associations, and other organizations that lobbies for immigration reforms to facilitate the hiring of foreign workers by U.S. companies. The coalition supports a guest worker program to bring in foreign workers legally and programs to allow undocumented workers already in the United States to earn legal status. The group's Web site contains press releases and other information relevant to this issue.

## Federation for American Immigration Reform (FAIR)

25 Massachusetts Avenue NW, Suite 300
Washington, DC 20001
(202) 328-7004 • fax: (202) 387-3447
e-mail: comments@fairus.org
Web site: www.fairus.org

The Federation for American Immigration Reform (FAIR) is a national, nonprofit, public interest membership organization of concerned citizens dedicated to reforming the nation's immigration policies and slowing or stopping illegal immigration. FAIR seeks to improve border security, to stop illegal immigration, and to reduce annual immigration levels to about 300,000. FAIR's Web site contains publications on illegal immigration including reports such as *Amnesty and the Economy: Myths, Lies, and Obfuscation* and *The Costs of Illegal Immigration to Floridians.*

## Heritage Foundation

214 Massachusetts Avenue NE, Washington, DC 20002-4999
(202) 546-4400 • fax: (202) 546-8328
Web site: www.heritage.org

The Heritage Foundation is a public policy research organization that advocates for conservative policies based on the principles of individual freedom, free enterprise, limited government, a strong national defense, and traditional American values. The group favors secure borders and strong enforcement of U.S. immigration laws, and it opposes amnesty for illegal immigrants. Its Web site contains research papers on illegal immigration, including *Amnesty as an Economic Stimulus: Not the Answer to the Illegal Immigration Problem* and *Help the Economy and Federal Deficit by Raising H-1B Caps.*

**Mexican American Legal Defense and Educational Fund (MALDEF)**

1016 Sixteenth Street NW, Washington, DC 20036
(202) 293-2828
Web site: www.maldef.org

The Mexican American Legal Defense and Educational Fund (MALDEF) is a nonprofit Latino litigation, advocacy, and educational outreach institution. MALDEF is dedicated to safeguarding the civil rights of Latinos in the United States and empowering the Latino community to fully participate in U.S. society. MALDEF's Immigrants' Rights program seeks to protect the rights of immigrants through litigation and legislative advocacy. Its Web site lists publications relevant to immigration, including *Guiding Principles for Comprehensive Immigration Reform.*

**Minuteman Project**

PO Box 3944, Laguna Hills, CA 92654
(949) 587-5199
Web site: www.minutemanproject.com

The Minuteman Project is a grassroots volunteer organization with local chapters that advocate for enforcement of U.S. immigration laws and halting illegal immigration. The group's Web site contains press releases and other information about the group's activities and the illegal immigration issue. Recent publications include *California: Mexico's Maternity Ward* and *U.S. Taxpayer Funding Education of Mexican Children.*

### National Council of La Raza (NCLR)

1126 Sixteenth Street NW, Raul Yzaguirre Building
Washington, DC   20036
(202) 785-1670 • fax: (202) 776-1792
e-mail: comments@nclr.org
Web site: www.nclr.org

The National Council of La Raza (NCLR) is a national Hispanic civil rights and advocacy organization that works to improve opportunities for Hispanic Americans. NCLR conducts
research, policy analysis, and advocacy to provide a Latino
perspective in five key areas—assets/investments, education,
employment and economic status, health, and civil rights/
immigration. NCLR's Web site provides analysis on immigration legislation and various publications relevant to the illegal
immigration debate. Some examples include *Five Facts About
Undocumented Workers in the United States* and *Paying the
Price: The Impact of Immigration Raids on America's Children.*

### National Immigration Forum

50 F Street NW, Suite 300, Washington, DC   20001
(202) 347-0040 • fax: (202) 347-0058
Web site: www.immigrationforum.org

The National Immigration Forum is an immigrants' rights organization dedicated to promoting public policies that welcome immigrants and refugees. It advocates for generous immigration policies that are supportive of newcomers to the
United States. The forum's Web site contains press releases, a
blog, and other publications, such as *Change and Continuity:
Public Opinion on Immigration Reform* and *Harnessing the Ad-
vantages of Immigration for a 21st-Century Economy.*

### National Network for Immigrant and
### Refugee Rights (NNIRR)

310 Eighth Street, Suite 303, Oakland, CA   94607
(510) 465-1984 • fax: (510) 465-1885
e-mail: nnirr@nnirr.org
Web site: www.nnirr.org

The National Network for Immigrant and Refugee Rights (NNIRR) is a national organization composed of local coalitions and immigrant, refugee, community, religious, civil rights, and labor organizations and activists. It seeks to educate the public about immigration issues and promotes U.S. immigration policies that protect the rights of all immigrants and refugees, regardless of immigration status. Recent publications include *Over-Raided, Under Siege: US Immigration Laws and Enforcement Destroy the Rights of Immigrants.*

## NumbersUSA

1601 North Kent Street, Suite 1100, Arlington, VA   22209
(703) 816-8820
Web site: www.numbersusa.com

NumbersUSA is a nonprofit, nonpartisan, public policy organization that opposes high levels of immigration and seeks to educate the public about immigration numbers. The organization favors an environmentally sustainable and economically just America. The group's Web site features a blog and articles about illegal immigration and other immigration issues. Recent publications include *The Case Against Immigration* and *With Jobless Rates Like These, How Can Anybody Consider More Foreign Workers or an Amnesty?*

## Pew Hispanic Center

1615 L Street NW, Suite 700, Washington, DC   20036-5610
(202) 419-3600 • fax: (202) 419-3608
e-mail: info@pewhispanic.org
Web site: http://pewhispanic.org

The Pew Hispanic Center is a nonpartisan research organization with a mission to improve understanding of the U.S. Hispanic population and to chronicle Latinos' growing impact on the nation. The center does not take positions on policy issues, but it has published numerous reports and research studies on immigration topics, including *Hispanics and the Criminal Justice System: Low Confidence, High Exposure* and *A Portrait of Unauthorized Immigrants in the United States.*

## Service Employees International Union (SEIU)
1800 Massachusetts Avenue NW, Washington, DC   20036
(800) 424-8592
Web site: www.seiu.org

The Service Employees International Union (SEIU) represents workers in hospitals, long-term care facilities, property services, and public services. It advocates for immigration reforms to improve conditions for immigrant workers. SEIU's Web site contains position papers and other publications, including *Immigrant Workers: Making Valuable Contributions to Our Communities and Our Economy.*

## U.S. Citizenship and Immigration Services (USCIS)
20 Massachusetts Avenue NW, Washington, DC   20529
(800) 375-5283
Web site: www.uscis.gov

The U.S. Citizenship and Immigration Services (USCIS) is part of the U.S. Department of Homeland Security (DHS). USCIS replaced the former U.S. Immigration and Naturalization Service (INS), which was abolished on March 1, 2003, and it is charged with processing immigrant visa petitions and providing other immigration services. The USCIS Web site contains links to immigration enforcement entities, including the U.S. Immigration and Customs Enforcement (ICE) and the U.S. Customs and Border Protection (CBP).

## United States Conference of Catholic Bishops (USCCB)
3211 Fourth Street NE, Washington, DC   20017
(202) 541-3000
Web site: www.usccb.org

The United States Conference of Catholic Bishops (USCCB) is an assembly of Catholic bishops who work to unify, coordinate, promote, and carry on Catholic activities in the United States. One of the group's priorities is helping immigrants, and the USCCB advocates for amnesty to legalize the millions of illegal immigrants living in the United States. Its Web site provides information about immigration issues, including publications such as *How Should an Undocumented Foreign National Prepare Now for Legalization?*

# Bibliography

## Books

Ann Bausum — *Denied, Detained, Deported: Stories from the Dark Side of American Immigration*. Washington, DC: National Geographic Children's Books, 2009.

Jagdish Bhagwati and Gordon Hanson — *Skilled Immigration Today: Prospects, Problems, and Policies*. New York: Oxford University Press, 2009.

Ilona M. Bray, Jeptha Evans, and Ruby Lieberman — *U.S. Immigration Made Easy*. Berkeley, CA: Nolo Press, 2009.

Patrick J. Buchanan — *State of Emergency: The Third World Invasion and Conquest of America*. New York: St. Martin's Press, 2006.

Justin Akers Chacón and Mike Davis — *No One Is Illegal: Fighting Violence and State Repression on the U.S.-Mexico Border*. Chicago: Haymarket Books, 2006.

Jim Gilchrist and Jerome R. Corsi — *Minutemen: The Battle to Secure America's Borders*. Los Angeles, CA: World Ahead Publishing, 2006.

J.D. Hayworth — *Whatever It Takes: Illegal Immigration, Border Security, and the War on Terror*. Washington, DC: Regnery Publishers, Inc., 2006.

Paul W. Hickman and Thomas P. Curtis, eds.
*Immigration Crisis: Issues, Policies and Consequences.* New York: Nova Science Publishers, 2008.

Bill Ong Hing
*Deporting Our Souls: Values, Morality, and Immigration Policy.* New York: Cambridge University Press, 2006.

Samuel L. Huntington
*Who Are We?: The Challenges to America's National Identity.* New York: Simon & Shuster, 2004.

Mark Krikorian
*The New Case Against Immigration: Both Legal and Illegal.* New York: Sentinel HC, 2008.

William McDonald
*Immigration, Crime and Justice.* United Kingdom: Emerald Group Publishing Limited, 2009.

Tony Payan
*The Three U.S.-Mexico Border Wars: Drugs, Immigration, and Homeland Security.* Westport, CT: Praeger Security International, 2006.

Stanley A. Renshon
*The 50% American: Immigration and National Identity in an Age of Terror.* Washington, DC: Georgetown University Press, 2005.

Matthew Soerens, Jenny Hwang, and Leith Anderson
*Welcoming the Stranger: Justice, Compassion & Truth in the Immigration Debate.* Downers Grove, IL: IVP Books, 2009.

Tom Tancredo
*In Mortal Danger: The Battle for America's Border and Security.* Nashville, TN: WND Books, 2006.

## Periodicals

*Economist*            "All Together Now: Could This Be
                       the Year for Immigration Reform?"
                       April 16, 2009.

Thomas R.              "Myth vs. Fact: Politicians and
Eddlem                 Pundits Are Defending Illegal
                       Immigration with Worn-Out Myths
                       That Can Easily Be Proven Wrong,"
                       *New American*, May 1, 2006.

Mallory Factor         "A Better Way: Enforcement Can't
                       Solve Our Immigration Woes, but
                       Neither Can Amnesty," *National
                       Review*, April 27, 2009.

Moira Herbst           "A Makeover for Immigration
                       Policy?" *Business Week*, May 1, 2009.

William P. Hoar        "Sham Stances on Illegal
                       Immigration," *New American*,
                       October 16, 2006.

Tamar Jacoby           "Immigration Nation," *Foreign
                       Affairs*, November-December 2006.

Stephen Johnson        "The Best Immigration Reform;
                       Stimulating Growth South of the
                       Border Will Stem the Tide of Illegal
                       Aliens," *Business Week*, April 24, 2006.

*Judicial Watch*       "Napolitano Cancels Immigration
                       Enforcement Operations," March 30,
                       2009. www.judicialwatch.org.

Kristi Keck            "Immigration Reform: Will the
                       Climate Ever Be Right?" CNN.com,
                       April 10, 2009. www.cnn.com.

Jim Kessler          "Tough, Fair and Practical: Solving
                     the Immigration Wedge," *Campaigns
                     & Elections*, October-November 2006.

Cort Kirkwood        "Illegal Immigration: Immigration
                     Protests Are Spreading Across
                     America. What Is the Motive? What
                     Is the Agenda?" *New American*, May
                     1, 2006.

Maria L.             "Our Town—Or Is It Theirs?" *Los
La Ganga             Angeles Times*, September 19, 2006.

Richard S. Lefrak    "Immigrants Can Help Fix the
and A. Gary          Housing Bubble," *Wall Street Journal*,
Shilling             March 17, 2009.

Roger Lowenstein     "The Immigration Equation," *New
                     York Times Magazine*, July 9, 2006.

Heather              "Seeing Today's Immigrants Straight,"
Mac Donald           *City Journal*, Summer 2006.

Heather              "What Would Mexico Do with
Mac Donald           Protesting Illegals?" *City Journal*,
                     April 10, 2006.

*National            "Churches Take Immigration Reform
Catholic Reporter*   Fight into the Streets," March 31,
                     2006.

*National            "The Immigration Dilemma,"
Catholic Reporter*   January 13, 2006.

*New York Times*     "A Shift on Immigration," May 2,
                     2009.

William Plasencia,   "Immigration Is Needed," *South
ed.                  Florida CEO*, May 2006.

| | |
|---|---|
| Julia Preston | "Obama to Push Immigration Bill as One Priority," *New York Times*, April 8, 2009. |
| Julia Preston and Steven Greenhouse | "Immigration Accord by Labor Boosts Obama Effort," *New York Times*, April 13, 2009. |
| Michelle Roberts | "Analysis Shows How Illegal Immigrants Face Long Detention and Have Few Rights," Associated Press, March 16, 2009. |
| Greg Simmons | "Immigration's Effect on Economy Is Murky," FOXNews, March 30, 2006. www.foxnews.com. |
| Daniel B. Wood | "In Hard Times, Illegal Immigrants Lose Healthcare," *Christian Science Monitor*, March 24, 2009. |
| Byron York | "Illegal Immigrants, Unite! And Under the Union Banner, Too," *National Review*, May 8, 2006. |

# Index